Hell's Abyss, Heaven's Grace

Hell's Abyss, Heaven's Grace

WAR AND CHRISTIAN SPIRITUALITY

Lawrence D. Hart

Cowley Publications
CAMBRIDGE, MASSACHUSETTS

Published in the United States of America by Cowley Publications, a division of the Society of Saint John the Evangelist. No portion of this book may be reproduced, stored in or introduced into a retrieval system, or transmitted, in any form or by any means— including photocopying—without the prior written permission of Cowley Publications, except in the case of brief quotations embedded in critical articles and reviews.

Library of Congress Control No:
2005031669

ISBN-10: 1-56101-241-6
ISBN-13: 978-1-56101-241-1

Unless otherwise noted, scripture quotations are taken from the New Revised Standard Version of the Bible, © 1989, by the Division of Christian Education of the National Council of the Churches of Christ in the United States of America. Used by permission.

CEV: The Contemporary English Version Copyright © 1995 by American Bible Society. Used by permission.

MESSAGE: *The Message*. Copyright © 1993, 1994, 1995, 1996, 2000, 2001, 2002. Used by permission of NavPress Publishing Group.

NASB: Scripture taken from the New American Standard Bible®. Copyright © 1960, 1962, 1963, 1968, 1971, 1972, 1973, 1975, 1977, 1995 by The Lockman Foundation. Used by permission.

NIV: The Holy Bible, New International Version®. Copyright © 1973, 1978, 1984, International Bible Society. Used by permission of Zondervan. All rights reserved.

Cover design: Gary Ragaglia
Cover art: *Harvest Moon* by Sherridan Smith, www.smsmith.com
Interior design: Wendy Holdman

This book was printed in the United States of America on acid-free paper.

Cowley Publications
4 Brattle Street
Cambridge, Massachusetts 02138
800-225-1534 • www.cowley.org

The only people on earth who do not see Christ and his teachings as nonviolent are Christians.

MOHANDAS K. GANDHI

For our grandchildren

Dashiell, Autumn, Asher, and Camille

the peace of God which passes all understanding
keep their hearts and minds in Christ Jesus.

∿

Contents

Introduction

War, before it is ever manifested in physical, observable violence, and peace, before it is ever felt as harmony or seen in acts of kindness, are the inner realities of the human heart and mind. They are states of consciousness, conditions of the soul. It is as the seventeenth-century poet and mystic Angelus Silesius wrote:

> In you is hell's abyss, in you is heaven's grace,
> What you elect and want you have in any place.[1]

War is "hell's abyss," and peace is "heaven's grace." Moment by moment we choose which we will live into; indeed, which we will become. E. Stanley Jones, an extraordinary Christian who was nominated five times for the Nobel Peace Prize and counted Mahatma Gandhi among his good friends, began one of his explorations of Christian thought and practice with this observation: "The outer arrangements of humanity are awry because the inner arrangements of humanity are awry. For the whole of the outer arrangements of life rest upon the inner. Men and women cannot get along with each other because they cannot get along with themselves, and they cannot get along with themselves because they cannot get along with God."[2] What Jones wrote in the middle of the twentieth century is as appropriate now as it was then. He was pointing to the dynamics of spiritual principles that are always and everywhere true. "The breakdown [in 'international comity']," he said, "is due to a breakdown in something back behind the economic and political—a breakdown in the spiritual. Something has collapsed there, and the outer collapse is simply an outer expression of a more serious inner collapse."[3]

To be Christian is to believe that everything, absolutely everything—our happiness, our sanity, our life—is determined by our spiritual orientation. We can certainly live, as do countless individuals and nations, as if there is no spiritual realm, no life to be lived in the Spirit, and no soul to be nurtured. But if we do, there is eventually some sort of inner collapse into futility. "But what happens when we live God's way?" asks Saint Paul, who goes on to answer his own question: "God brings gifts into our lives, much the same way that fruit appears in an orchard— things like affection for others, exuberance about life, serenity. We develop a willingness to stick with things, a sense of compassion in the heart, and a conviction that a basic holiness permeates things and people. We find ourselves involved in loyal commitments, not needing to force our way in life, able to marshal and direct our energies wisely" (Galatians 5:22, MESSAGE).

The spiritual life is a life of communion, or presence—of being in God. A woman once approached a monk known for his serenity and wisdom and asked for help with her spiritual practice. The monk gave her a sieve and a cup, and led her down to the seashore and out on a rock, the water splashing and swirling around them. "Show me," he said to her, "how you fill the sieve with water." She bent down, dipped the cup into the water and poured the water into the sieve. But no matter how quickly or how often she repeated this action the water would barely appear at the bottom of the sieve and then it was gone. Finally the monk said to her, "That's not the way to fill the sieve with water, or the self with divine life." He gently took the sieve from her and threw it as far as he could into the sea. It briefly floated on the surface and then sank into the water. With that she realized that the sieve was in the water and now full of water. "This is the way of spiritual practice," the monk said. "It is not pouring little cupfuls of divine life into the individual person, but casting ourselves far out into the sea of divine life so that we are in God and God is in us." So Saint Paul said to the Athenian philosophers, "It is in God that we live, move and have our being" (Acts 17:28).

Peace is often thought of as the absence of conflict, but peace is not absence—it is Presence. It is being in the mystical, but very real, presence of Spirit. Peace is *being in Love.* Selfishness, greed, hatred, and war are evil because they are antithetical to being, loving, and *being in love.* In the first two chapters of this book, I will try to show that wherever there is a fork in our path the only choice available to those who have given themselves over to the creative energy of extravagant Love is the way of peace. I believe that the Spirit of Christ is all-pervading and that where the Spirit is, there is truth, justice, and mercy.

Chapters 3 and 4 are intended to demonstrate that just war theory is an illusion—a myth developed to rationalize the violence human beings do against one another. Chapter 3, "America and the Holy War Myth," examines the holy or just war within the context of American history. I understand, of course, that "America" and "the United States" are not synonyms and that all people who inhabit the American Continent are Americans. However, in this book I have used "America" and "American" as commonly, if too narrowly, understood by most of the people in my country—especially by those whose dreams are filled with visions of empire. Chapter 4, "Demythologizing the War in Iraq," looks at the theory in light of the U.S.-led invasion and occupation of Iraq. In fact, throughout this book specific reference is frequently made to the war in Iraq. As the most recent and familiar military conflict to Americans it provides an apt case study.

Chapter 5, "Confronting the Hypothetical Dilemma," enters into the question raised throughout John Howard Yoder's book *What Would You Do? A Serious Answer to a Standard Question.*[4]

When I told people I was writing a book with the working title of *The Conscience of a Christian Pacifist,* they often responded by saying they could not embrace pacifism because they knew they would be willing to kill in order to protect their family. This is the issue that Yoder examines. The problem is usually phrased in this rather sexist fashion: "What would you do if an armed madman was attacking your wife (or daughter, or sister, or grandmother) and you had a gun?" If you answer that you would kill the attacker, you have supposedly proven that you do not really believe in pacifism and that you are contradicting your stated opposition to war and commitment to nonviolence. If, on the other hand, you are unwilling to immediately shoot the aggressor dead, it is argued that you are morally irresponsible in refusing to protect the innocent by killing another person. It is my hope that, by reexamining Yoder's careful and logical analysis of the question, readers will see the further implication that the virtues of humility, integrity, compassion, and truth are proven only as they confront and are confronted by egoism, hatred, and mendacity.

The conclusion brings everything full circle by framing the problem of human violence as essentially moral and spiritual. It posits Christian contemplative practice as a way out of our madness.

There is also an application section entitled "A Different Road Map to Peace." It was originally a short essay on the violence between Israel and Palestine. It was offered as a commentary piece to a national church paper but was rejected as "too hot to publish." I include it here as an elaboration on certain assertions I make earlier in this book. I also include it because I see no way to peace in the Middle East without honestly confronting the role of Israel and the United States in the awful cycle of violence in that ancient and—to Jews, Christians, and Muslims—sacred land. I hope that by addressing this very specific contemporary situation, these final thoughts will remind us that we must seek peace now, everywhere, and always.

Much of what is written here may seem too political to many of my fellow Christians. The deeper we go into contemplative prayer, however, the deeper we grow in compassion and in our communion with God and the whole of humanity. In his poem "The Rime of the Ancient Mariner," Samuel Taylor Coleridge gave a wonderful sense of how communion with God is affected by our practice of an all-embracing love:

> He prayeth best, who loveth best
> All things both great and small;
> For the dear God who loveth us,
> He made and loveth all.[5]

It is quite impossible to lead a religious, or spiritual, life of depth without identifying ourselves with the entire human race and the cosmos that we inhabit. Peace, the Hebrew *shalom,* leaves nothing and no one out. Consequently the "blessed peacemakers" of the Beatitudes, like the ancient prophets, are concerned with social, economic, and political justice—not justice in the sense of giving someone the punishment we think they deserve, but justice in the biblical sense of championing the cause of the vulnerable. In the little Epistle of Saint James (paraphrased for the sake of emphasis), the author writes: "In the sight of God real religion, the most beautiful liturgy in which you can participate, is to reach out a hand to the homeless and powerless and to love the unloved and unwanted" (James 1:27).

Nevertheless, what is written here should not be construed as advocating nonviolence or pacifism as a strategy for achieving political ends. Those who embrace nonviolence as external means to external ends are at risk of turning to violence as soon as there is opportunity, or when their frustration reaches what seems to them an intolerable level. Real peace is not a tactic, but what we are in our innermost being. Until we understand this we will not understand the core difference between war and peace. In *The Path of Peace,* Henri J. M. Nouwen asked this

incisive question: "When those who want peace are as interested in success, popularity, and power as those who want war,
what then is the real difference between war and peace? When
peace is as much of this world as war, what other choice is there
but the choice between a war we euphemistically call pacifica-
tion and a peace in which the peacemakers violate one another's
deepest values?"[6]

What is the difference? Nouwen's question is rhetorical.
When peace is as much of this world as war there is obviously
no difference. This pseudopeace and violence are just different
words for the same state of mind. But real peace and war are as
different as "hell's abyss and heaven's grace," and the difference
is in us.

· 1 ·

To Love as God Loves

"You have heard that it was said, 'You shall love your neighbor and hate your enemy.' But I say to you, Love your enemies and pray for those who persecute you, so that you may be children of your Father in heaven; for he makes his sun rise on the evil and on the good, and sends rain on the righteous and the unrighteous. For if you love those who love you, what reward do you have? Do not even the tax collectors do the same? And if you greet only your brothers and sisters, what more are you doing than others? Do not even the Gentiles do the same? Be perfect, therefore, as your heavenly Father is perfect."

MATTHEW 5:43–48

The Good Lord Loves You

Years ago, when I first heard Neil Diamond sing "The Good Lord Loves You," it resonated deep within me. And as I recall the lyrics now, they provide a valid interpretation and witness to Jesus' words as found in Matthew's Sermon on the Mount and a soulful commentary on the violence that is rampant in our world.

It is a song of both assurance and lament. It is sung for "junk-
ies and juicers," for those in our prisons and jails, for people who
have nowhere to go, and for every good person who nevertheless
fails to live the way they know is best. It is sung for all those politically involved, and for every man and woman in the military,
and for every mother and child trying to make it through this
world. The word of assurance is in the refrain: "The good Lord
loves you. The good Lord loves you. The good Lord loves you so."
But in the end a lament arises out of this word of reassurance and
comfort. It expresses a longing, sung with a feeling deep in the
heart, to "tear down the walls that keep us apart"; to tear down
the walls so that love and compassion can flow freely between us.
Then, at the end of the final refrain, the lament is put as a question whose answer evokes a great sorrow:

> The good Lord loves you
> He loves you so
> Ain't it sad that we're doing so bad.[1]

Those who belong to a religious order, monks and nuns, adopt
the rule of life for that order. The rule of life for every man and
every woman who embraces the teachings of Christ is to show
everyone they meet the same love, mercy, and compassion as
that of the God who loves the whole world like a nursing mother
or a wise and caring father. The more we know of the height,
the depth, and the breadth of God's love for us, the more we are
drawn to love all others—the good and the bad, those near and
those faraway—in the same way that we ourselves have been
loved.

This is the simple but unfathomably profound meaning of
Jesus' words in the Gospel according to Matthew. "Be perfect.
Be perfect as your heavenly Father is perfect." To be perfect obviously does not mean that we have come to a point of complete
flawlessness; nor does it mean that we have come to the end
of all possibilities for further growth. Rather, it is Jesus' way of

saying that because we have experienced the gratuitous love of God, because of who we are in Christ, because of our spiritual genetics, we should resemble God, not in our moral impeccability but in our undiscriminating, impartial, unconditional love. It is Jesus' way of saying that we should resemble God by loving not only our own families and friends and admirers and supporters and allies but by loving the enemy who would do us harm and the stranger whose ways seem odd and even alienating. Jesus challenges us to undergo the most radical kind of transformation, a metamorphosis, in order to love beyond all reasons to love—suffering willingly and creatively because that is what God is like.

In the Sermon on the Mount Jesus denies every calculation of human worth based on merit or personal preference. We are inclined to love our own, to love the lovable, to do good to those who do good to us, to lend to the reliable, to give to the grateful. Ultimately our attempts to justify violence and killing are based on an egocentric reckoning of human worth. So I am tempted to think that my little grandchildren are, precisely because they are mine, more precious than your children or grandchildren. But to the God who made us and loves us all, the nearly one million Iraqi children under the age of five who died because of U.S.-enforced sanctions (500,000 between 1991 and 1998 and 5,000–6,000 per month from 1998 to the beginning of the war in 2003)[2] and all the Iraqi children who have died, or who will die, directly or indirectly as a result of the American invasion of their country, are no less precious than my babies or your babies.

The Logic of Love

Recently one morning I read that in the heat of a scorching afternoon an Iraqi man, a husband and father, frantically approached Sergeant David Borell at a U.S. Army airfield, pleading for help for his three children, who had been badly burned after finding and setting fire to a bag of abandoned explosives.

Sgt. Borell immediately called for medical help but it was two hours before anyone came. Two Army doctors finally arrived on the scene but refused to help the three injured children. The injuries, the doctors said, were not life-threatening and were not inflicted by U.S. troops; they were therefore under no obligation to do anything. And that is what they did—nothing! This father's two little girls and his boy are covered with scabs, and his son cannot use his right leg.[3]

Someone once said that a person who does not believe that the Christian way is the way of nonviolence and compassion is an atheist. I don't know if, according to strict logic, that is completely true, but I do know without a shadow of doubt that if we don't believe in Christian nonviolence and compassion we fall far short of what Jesus calls us to be. No one who believes, even unconsciously, that the life of an American child is worth more than the life of an Iraqi, Iranian, North Korean, or Syrian child truly knows Christ. No one who callously ignores the suffering of any child, no one who brings suffering, devastation, and death to children, can legitimately claim to be a true follower of Jesus of Nazareth.

As incomprehensible as it may be to some people, the life of every man, woman, and child—in Iraq or anywhere else in this world—is as precious as their own life or the life of any member of their family. Many scholars have studied the moral, faith, and spiritual development of human beings just as others have studied intellectual and physical development. Our stages of spiritual development have been carefully delineated. If we are at that level of moral and spiritual development where we believe that good things really ought to happen to good people and bad things ought to happen to bad people, and we are confident that by definition we are the good guys, then Christ's words about loving our enemies will remain unintelligible and prove an embarrassment or even an offense to us.

The deeper our interior spiritual life, the greater our realization that we, though many, are part of a harmonious whole. So, as Barbara Brown Taylor observes, the mother who sits bolt upright in the middle of the night "knowing" something has happened to her child does so, not because of some psychic power, "but because they belong to the same unbroken wholeness of the universe."[4] The logic of unity is clear: I cannot hurt another without hurting myself. We are all the sons and daughters of Eve—"offspring" of the "one God and Father of all, who is above all and through all and in all" (Acts 17:28; Ephesians 4:6). Taylor visualizes this mystery as a "luminous web":

> There is another way to conceive of our life together. There is another way to conceive of our life in God, but it requires a different world view—not a clockwork universe in which individuals function as concrete springs and gears, but one that looks more like a luminous web, in which the whole is far more than the parts. In this universe there is no such thing as an individual apart from his or her relationships. Every interaction—between people and people, between people and things, between things and things—changes the face of history. . . . Our mental torture comes about only because we insist on conceiving of reality as many when it is truly and deeply one. All appearances to the contrary, "the universe remains as it was in the beginning, when all places where one place, all times one time, all things the same thing."[5]

Taylor goes on to explain that in this picture of reality as a "web of relationships—an infinite web, flung across the vastness of space like a luminous net" made of energy with light moving through it—God is the web, God is the energy, the space, and the light." She writes, "It is not enough to say that God is responsible for all this unity. Instead I want to proclaim that God is the unity."[6]

The saints among us are people whose lives are characterized by experiences of the Unity that runs through all things, and in which we "live and move and have our being" (Acts 17:28). In

the enlightenment that accompanies this sense of connected-
ness, we are transformed into the very ethical ideals we have
tried to enact. One does not merely become a peace advocate,
but the embodiment of peace. The twentieth-century Trappist
monk Thomas Merton told how in the middle of the shopping
district in Louisville, Kentucky, at the corner of 4th and Walnut,
he was suddenly overwhelmed by the realization that he was
one with all the people around him, and that he loved them. His
sense of separateness melted away and, in the heart of God, he
was one with the whole of humanity.[7]

Henri Nouwen tells this story of an old Rabbi:

> The rabbi asked his students: "How can we determine the
> hour of dawn, when the night ends and the day begins?"
>
> One of the rabbi's students suggested: "When from a
> distance you can distinguish between a dog and a sheep?"
>
> "No," was the answer of the rabbi.
>
> "Is it when one can distinguish between a fig tree and
> a grapevine?" asked a second student.
>
> "No," the rabbi said.
>
> "Please tell us the answer, then," said the students.
>
> "It is, then," said the wise teacher, "when you can look
> into the face of human beings and you have enough light
> [in you] to recognize them as your brothers and sisters.
> Up until then it is night, and darkness is still with us."[8]

Nouwen is absolutely right. It's when we can look into someone's face and see our common humanity, our essential solidarity, our brotherhood and sisterhood, that the peace of God
dawns within us.

The Ruin of Selfishness

On the same day that I read the story about the two doctors
and the burned children, I accidentally tuned into a religious

talk show (I cannot bring myself to call it Christian). One of the hosts said that the Iraqis are a wicked and barbaric people, and the only way to deal with them is barbarically. I cannot conceive of how any intelligent, feeling human being can harmonize such a thought with the teaching of Jesus:

> "You have heard that it was said, 'You shall love your neighbor and hate your enemy.' But I say to you, Love your enemies and pray for those who persecute you, so that you may be children of your Father in heaven; for he makes his sun rise on the evil and on the good, and sends rain on the righteous and on the unrighteous." (Matthew 5:43–45)

But it is, as Jesus also said, a narrow gate and an arduous path that leads to life and peace, and very few ever find it (Matthew 17:13, 14). In the East there is a similar saying: "The spiritual path is a razor's edge—hard to find and difficult to tread." Without a deep reverence for life and appreciation for the oneness that pervades all things, it is highly unlikely—although, considering God's grace, not impossible—that we will be able to find or to walk this path that leads us home to the heart of God.

It is the audacious claim of Christians that they have caught a glimpse, indeed, that they have been given a sacred vision, of what lies beyond the gate and down the path. For the prophet Micah it is a vision of peace and justice and perfect communion. It is a vision of a redeemed world. In fact, this vision of a redeemed world is constantly recurring, like a haunting melody that runs throughout Holy Scripture. The last verse of the first chapter of the Bible affirms a wonderful and lofty view of creation: "God saw everything that had been made and behold it was very good" (Genesis 1:31, NIV). If the world was created good, then God's desire must surely be to redeem, not to destroy, creation. And God's intention for each of us must be that we become a part of this redeeming, creative, transforming process that has been going on for ages and ages. Squandering natural resources on the weapons of war, polluting the earth by manufacturing and testing instruments of death, systematically destroying our planet in the interest of violence and greed, ignoring millions of people—especially the children who are without food or medicine or shelter—are all a rejection of the holy vision God has given us and blasphemy against the goodness of God's creation.

The details of our selfish life are daunting in their number and kind. The Pentagon produces one ton of toxic waste per minute. In fact, the U.S. military, which is responsible for one-third of this country's toxic waste, produces more hazardous waste annually than the five largest international chemical companies— 750,000 tons of lethal waste annually. Contamination due to the toxic waste produced by the military poisoned the only source of drinking water for a million people on Cape Cod, Massachusetts. Perchlorate, a chemical found in military munitions, has contaminated drinking water in eighteen states. Increased risk of lung cancer for women, low birth weights for infants, and clusters of childhood leukemia have been documented for families living near military bases.[9] In the process of creating new weapons and testing missiles, the Redstone Arsenal in Huntsville, Alabama, has heavily contaminated that installation's soil and water with solvents, metals, heavy metals, and semivolatile organics.[10] What is so frightening is that this lethal contamination cannot be contained—it spreads through runoff and groundwater. The 382,000-acre Naval Air Station in Jacksonville, Florida, is polluted with jet fuels, PCBs, and low-level radioactive waste.[11] The 918,000 acres of Fort Wainwright near Anchorage, Alaska, are contaminated by unexploded ordnance, chemical agents, and heavy metals.[12] At Fort Kelly Air Force Base in the heart of San Antonio, Texas, workers in an open warehouse cleaned radioactive uranium dust from dummy nuclear warheads. It is no surprise, of course, that those workers have had a high incidence of cancer. The nearby base at Medina has five radioactive sites and there are other locations that have not yet been acknowledged by the military.[13]

Depleted uranium is the residue left when natural uranium has been refined. It is used in bombs, artillery shells, and Gatling guns because of its ability to penetrate armor and other hard surfaces. The United States has used these munitions, which continue to kill long after the fighting is over, in Kosovo, Afghanistan, and Iraq. Arundhati Roy, in her book *War Talk,* writes: "American and British forces have fired thousands of missiles and bombs on Iraq. Iraq's fields and farmlands have been shelled with three hundred tons of depleted uranium. . . . In Southern Iraq, there has been a fourfold increase in cancer among children."[14] Roy's figures all predate Operation Iraqi Freedom. I do not understand, and I do not think that I ever will understand, how the military can say with a straight face that we do not make war on the innocent.

Yet one need not look beyond our own national borders to witness how limited and ruthless our community consciousness is. Thirty-seven million Americans live below the poverty line of $16,000 for a family of three and $19,000 for a family of four. Twelve million children live in families with incomes in this federally defined poverty, five million of them in families with incomes less than half the poverty level. All indications are that these numbers are rising. Research suggests that a family needs about twice that of the federal poverty level to meet its most essential needs. In 2004, 35 percent of the American people had to choose between buying food or paying their rent. Twenty-eight percent had to choose between medical care and eating. Thirteen million children live in families that must skip meals or eat less because they cannot afford to buy food. Statistics from 2000 show that more than three million men, women and children in the United States were homeless at some point in the year. Five million people, according to that data, spend half their income on housing, and consequently are always on the edge of homelessness; 20 percent of homeless people are employed; there are now American cities in which two people working for minimum wage cannot afford, with their incomes combined, to pay rent. Millions of elderly people are "food insecure." Jonathan Alter, writing in the September 19, 2005, issue of *Newsweek,* says "poverty in America is actually getting worse." In spite of three years of economic recovery 2004 saw a rise in poverty. The number of people living below the poverty level rose to 37 million, an increase of more than one million in one year. There are more poor people in the U.S. than the total population of Canada. Alter notes that the poverty rate in the U.S. (12.7 percent) "is the highest in the developed world and more than twice as high as in most other developed countries, which all strike a more generous contract with their weakest citizens."[15]

Our government is tight-fisted and shows little compassion for those who are hungry, or homeless, or who cannot afford basic medical care. Millions of people in the United States are without medical coverage.[16] Many of them, if someone in their family gets hurt or becomes ill, have to choose whether they will eat, pay rent, or seek medical attention. According to federal guidelines hospitals are allowed to screen out emergency room patients who are "stable"—that is, a patient who can walk out the door on his or her own—and the hospital does not have to provide that person with treatment. In order to save the millions that they would have to spend treating the working poor, the indigent, and the uninsured in their emergency rooms, hospitals tell those who can get off their beds and exit the hospital under their own power that they will have to pay or leave.[17]

With such need, where does the wealthiest nation in the world place its resources? The proposed military budget for 2004 was $399.1 billion—a $48 billion increase from the previous year. And to this we have added another $79 billion for six months of the war on Iraq. The United States, all by itself, accounts for half of the world's military spending—a strange use of resources for a peaceful nation. Projected military spending for 2005 amounted to $1.15 million a day, or $11,000 a second.[18] The estimated cost of the missile defense program proposed by President Bush is $1.2 trillion.[19]

While such massive funding could provide vital domestic support for millions of poor U.S. citizens, our country's leaders actually profit by waging war. Halliburton, the company Dick Cheney was CEO of just before becoming Vice President, has received what amounts to an unlimited contract for the rebuilding of Iraq.[20] Cheney will make about $1 million a year from Halliburton while vice president of the United States.[21] Every U.S. war will directly benefit Dick Cheney's bank account. Another company with close ties to our government's top brass, the Bechtel Corporation, will receive $1.7 billion for construction work in Iraq.[22] The membership of the Defense Advisory Board to the Pentagon is composed of retired admirals and generals now working as executives of Bechtel and Halliburton. The ties between the Pentagon and corporations like these are so close, their relationship can only be considered prostitution of the military or described as incestuous.[23] But no matter how you describe it, this is a system meant to make astronomical fortunes from killing, maiming, and destroying the homes of other human beings.

What makes our nation's military action particularly disturbing—indeed, evil—is that it is carried out under the guise of humanitarian motives and in the name of liberty. Invoking the name of democracy, our leaders have enriched themselves and neglected the poor. While lawmakers busily routed funds to promote our war in Iraq, there was a proposal to cut $61 million from child care for poor working families; $395 million from Head Start; $684 million in job training for workers and youth; $305 million from public housing, energy, and security; $172 million from health resources; $340 million from the Centers for Disease Control; $286 million from the Environmental Protection Agency; and $1.4 trillion to be diverted from Social Security to pay for other programs.[24]

The president's budget proposal for 2005 eliminates sixty-five programs, including housing, job training, and education programs that are important to low-income people. There is no help or relief in the proposal for the 44 million without health care or the 8.4 million without jobs. The president's proposal contains a $1.5 billion cut in federal funding for Medicaid. Failure to increase the Child Care and Development Block Grant by at least the rate of inflation means that more than 200,000 low-income parents will likely lose access to affordable child care. This is in addition to the 100,000 children denied care last year. The proposal for funding the No Child Left Behind legislation falls short of what is needed by $7.2 billion. Low-income housing will be cut by $900 million, eliminating 250,000 families from the program.

After the release of President Bush's proposed budget for 2006 some 300 religious leaders rallied in an ecumenical protest. Frank T. Griswold, Presiding Bishop of the Episcopal Church, observed that "budgets are moral documents" and that the spending plans of this $2.6 trillion budget "do not reflect gospel priorities." Others condemned the proposed budget as "in opposition to biblical values."[25] The cuts, whether considered from the perspective of the president's proposal or the Senate's plan, will adversely affect virtually all domestic programs, including veterans' benefits, education, environmental programs, housing programs, and health care.[26] The already precarious security of millions of families will be further jeopardized. Although the Republican-controlled Senate appeared to resist the president's unconscionable cuts to Medicaid, the Senate's plan would still cut $11 billion from the Medicaid program from 2006 to 2011. We appear doomed to a budget that raises taxes on the poorest workers, cuts taxes for the wealthy, and reduces crucial help and services to the poor who so desperately need them.[27] Sadly— and predictably—the list of ways we have turned our backs on the most vulnerable of our neighbors does not end here. There is more to consider.

Of the world's one hundred largest economies, fifty are not countries but corporations.[28] Increasingly, huge international corporations rule the world. Although not everyone is agreed on the terminology that best describes this expansion of corporate power, many observers refer to it as "globalization." The profit motive, with its dominant concerns of trade and investment, has become the driving force for the entire planet. There can be little doubt that globalization results in the denial of human dignity and justice. The use of slave labor, the exploitation of the poor, and the toxic contamination of the environment are a renunciation of the sacredness of work and the holy obligation to care for the environment.

The flourishing of international corporations has meant the exploitation of the poor and the deepening of their poverty—yes, even by Disneyland.[29] As unthinkable as it sounds to most Americans, Unicol, a U.S.-based corporation, has used slave labor to build a pipeline in Burma.[30] Cruel and bloody regimes are tolerated, even supported, as long as they serve Western corporate interests. Indeed, the U.S. military is the steel fist that enforces the greedy demands of big business.[31] In America itself, the plight and the number of the poor increase continually. For example, in 2003 "the number of Americans in poverty rose by 1.3 million to 35.9 million, or one in eight people. The number of Americans without health insurance rose by another 1.4 million to 45 million, or 15.6% of the population."[32] At the end of the day, the wealthy count their profits from war while the poor pay the costs. In his book *On Power and Ideology,* Noam Chomsky comments:

An analysis of imperial systems reveals costs as well as profits, perhaps often comparable in scale, some studies indicate. Why then should great powers seek to control an empire (classical or neoclassical)? In terms of the mysticism of "national interest," the policy seems to make little sense. It makes a good deal of sense however, when we reflect that the costs are social costs while the benefits are private benefits. The costs . . . are paid by the general population of the imperial society. The profits go to investors, exporters, banks, commercial institutions, agribusiness and the like. The empire is just one of the many devices by which the poor subsidize the wealthy in the home society.[33]

How America treats its poor demonstrates with terrible clarity the truthfulness of Chomsky's remarks. No repetition is sufficient to speak the crime. Exploiting the poor, desecrating the good earth in order to further dominance of the world by violence, and callously ignoring the often desperate needs of others as a guiding principle are egregious moral offenses to humanity and an abomination to God.

Manifestations of Love

Violence of every kind is an abomination. Divine love is the only power capable of healing creation and redeeming humankind from hell's abyss. The meaning of love, as even casual observation shows us, has been greatly distorted by the abuse of the word. But even if this were not true, the experience of love always defies any definitive description. The best we can do is to feel its artful contours in the same way that we might feel the beauty of a sculpture by running our hands over its elegant shape. The boundaries of love, as John Macquarrie notes, "cannot be precisely determined" because love "turns out to have such depth and inexhaustibility that the more we explore it the more we see that something further remains to be explored."[34] Nevertheless, an introductory reflection on the four ancient Greek words for love may be helpful for opening ourselves to a more intuitive, or contemplative, understanding of love and its power to save us.

Storgos

The word *storgos,* "natural affection," appears in Romans 1:31 as *astorgos,* meaning "without natural affection," and in Romans 12:10 as *philostorgos,* which might be rendered as "kindly

affectioned"—"love one another with mutual affection," as the
NRSV puts it. Since "kind" is originally *kinned*, "kindly affectioned" is having the affection of kindred.[35] Affection is experienced as a fond attachment, or kindly feeling toward another.
When you see a mother cat licking her baby kittens, that is natural affection. And when a mother eagerly takes her newborn
child into her arms, that is affection. When people are without natural affection we are understandably horrified. A young
woman in our community went into the dirty bathroom of a gas
station and, after giving birth to a baby boy in the toilet, drove
off in her car. Where there is no natural affection we know that
something is incomprehensibly wrong. A lack of affection may
threaten the very survival of the species. Without any affection
for kindred, the family is in danger. But Saint Paul said to the
Athenian philosophers that we are all God's "offspring" (Acts
17:28). When I was growing up, one of the worst things my
mother thought she could say about someone was "They have
no feelings." By that she meant that they seemed to feel no ten-
derness or fondness for others, especially for those in trouble.
She meant that there was some horrible deficiency in their character, and that deficiency was a lack of natural compassion. A
little affection for our kindred, for humanity in general, would
probably be helpful for reducing the violence in our world.

Eros

Eros may be thought of as love for what is beautiful. Because
of its association with sexual attraction, it has, unfortunately,
come into the English language as "erotic" and "erotica" with
their highly sexualized connotations. For many people the word
erotic is synonymous with *pornographic*. But in the Bible the
sensuality of love is regarded as a natural reality that can bless
and enrich life. The Song of Solomon celebrates the mysterious
intensity of sexual intimacy and sensual beauty. The bride's
breasts are soft and caressable like twin fawns. Her hips are

like rounded jewels. She is physically desirable, and her spirit is beautiful. Her neck is like the tower of David. The position of her neck, the way she carries herself, indicates strength and integrity of character. The groom also is handsome and pleasant. The bride says that his perfumes are pleasing, "and perfume poured forth is your name. Therefore the maidens love you" (Song of Solomon 1:3, *A Song for Lovers*). In the ancient Hebrew culture a person's name often expressed something about his or her character. As S. Craig Glickman observes in *A Song for Lovers:* "So when she said that his name was 'perfume poured forth,' she meant that his character was as fragrant and refreshing as cologne poured out of a bottle. This is the reason that the girls around the palace loved him—not just because he was handsome though he was, but because his inner person was so attractive."[36] In this love there is passion, and there is respect. In the Hebrew Scriptures the same word is used for both sexual and nonsexual love. This must mean that the element common to both usages, finding pleasure in another and attempting to overcome the distance between two people, was so strong that writers did not feel a need for different words.[37] By the time of Christ, *eros* as an attraction to physical beauty had been spiritualized so as to serve as a metaphor for spiritual and mystical encounters and also for the love of truth, because truth is beautiful. Psalm 27 expresses the passion, articulates the longing, of every contemplative soul:

> One thing I asked of the LORD,
>   that will I seek after:
> to live in the house of the LORD
>   all the days of my life,
> to behold the beauty of the LORD,
>   and to inquire in his temple. (Psalm 27:4)

To love and worship God is to be drawn into the transcendent beauty of God. It is to love God completely and passionately.

But that is not all. If we see God, if we see the ineffable beauty of God, we will also see the beauty of those around us (1 John 4:20). The poet Robinson Jeffers once wrote this wonderful line: "In the enormous invulnerable beauty of things, is the face of God."[38] Just imagine how it might change our world if we could see the beauty of God and of our planet and of all those who live on it.

Phileo

Phileo is usually characterized as the love that exists between friends. It is sometimes explained as a love that is based on mutual appreciation and interests. But I like the definition given in the *Theological Dictionary of the New Testament* better: "It means the love which embraces everything that bears a human countenance."[39] Just before Jesus was seized by the mob on that first Maundy Thursday, he told his disciples: "I'm no longer calling you servants because servants don't understand what their master is thinking and planning. No, I've named you friends because I've let you in on everything I've heard from the Father" (John 15:14–15, MESSAGE). It strikes me as particularly significant that Jesus is the one who initiates and extends friendship. The question, therefore, is not Who is my friend? but Whose friend can I be? Jesus explains in this same passage that we show our love for our friends when we put our lives on the line for them. Not many of us will ever be called on literally to die for someone, but we probably will be called to put our lives on the line by speaking and acting on behalf of the poor and oppressed in spite of the personal costs—socially, and perhaps economically as well.

Agape

Agape is a free and definite decision to act in a particular way toward others. It is a choice to treat others with civility, patience, kindness, humility, courtesy, generosity, forgiveness, and genuine good will, and to do so extravagantly:

> Love is kind and patient,
> never jealous, boastful,
> proud, or rude.
> Love isn't selfish
> or quick tempered.
> It doesn't keep a record
> of wrongs that others do.
> Love rejoices in the truth,
> but not in evil.
> Love is always supportive,
> loyal, hopeful,
> and trusting.
> Love never fails!
> (1 Corinthians 13:4–8, CEV)

The *Disciples of Christ in Community* teaching manual has one of the best definitions of *agape* that I have come across: "*Agape* is the type of love in which the motive is to respond to the legitimate needs of others without trying to get one's own needs met."[40] Notice that *agape* is free of the kind of neurosis that says, "You must let me love you" or "Life will be unbearable if you don't love me." *Agape* doesn't try to fix everything for anyone. It sees a particular legitimate need and responds appropriately where it has the capacity to do so. Because it is not based on emotion, *agape* does not require us to have warm feelings before we can act in the best interest of someone else. It is unconditional in that its determination to do others good does not depend in any way on who they are, on their personal qualities, on what they have done, or on what their disposition toward us has been. Love is creative. It can bring into being what did not previously exist—peace, hope, trust, and health. Violence and enmity can only destroy because evil can only react to what is already there. By the grace of God we all have the power to act creatively, regardless of our circumstances, to make this world a more peaceful, gentle, hospitable place. We can love. We can consecrate ourselves to love graciously, generously, and comprehensively without reservations or restrictions. We will never reach the end of love in this life. We will never come to the place where the practice of love may not be deepened. Hope for the world's salvation is rooted in our growth in love.

Thinking about the Greek vocabulary for love, about these four manifestations of love, can take us only so far. Experiencing divine love includes all of these expressions and much more. Astronauts have brought back rocks and soil from the moon. These artifacts give skilled scientists a good deal of information about the moon and answer many questions. But they also raise countless other questions. They do not fully explain or define the moon. Divine love is at last indefinable, inexplicable, incomprehensible. As Gerald May, psychiatrist and spiritual director, observes:

> No matter how experienced and knowledgeable we may be, we will always be children in the face of divine love. It will take us and turn us in ways we can never predict. And yet through our defensiveness and willful self-service we can place ourselves in opposition to it. Our fundamental choice then, is to oppose it or to be willing for it to happen. In this regard, the experience we have in different kinds of loving can indeed help us. It is not that through learning the nuances of erotic and filial love we become achievers of divine love, nor even that we become better recipients. We simply are able to increase our willingness. Deepening willingness is the only thing we can "do," the only "how to" of the entire process. This may seem like a very small degree of power to be gained from all the agony and struggle that goes into the experience of

loving, and in the universal sense it is indeed small. But if it is all we can do, then for each individual perhaps it is very significant. In the last analysis it may be the most significant thing in life.[41]

I think May is absolutely correct. In the end the most significant thing we can do, as co-creators with God, is to increase our willingness, our openness to divine love.

The Chance to Change

The miracle stories in the Bible are not for the sole benefit of the particular person helped or healed in them. Miracles (or "signs," as the Gospel of John prefers to call them) reveal something significant about the character or nature of God. In that way they are for the common spiritual good. Faith enables us to penetrate the mystery of a miracle. And the miracle of miracles is God's love for us. The great question that addresses each of us is whether that miracle will be lost on us.

My father was killed in an automobile accident when I was thirteen years old. I was filled with rage. I could be sitting anywhere—at my desk in school, in the pew at church, riding on the bus or in the car, appearing outwardly calm. But inwardly, wave after wave of maniacal fury would sweep through me. I wanted to smash, to pulverize everything around me. I wanted to hit someone. I didn't care what they did to me. I just wanted one good blow. I created opportunities for fights. I carried knives and brass knuckles to school. I was insane with rage. Spiritually and emotionally, I was in a little boat on a writhing sea of grief and anger. My face, the very way I looked, frightened people.

Then, slowly, in the bitter and disillusioned ground of my heart, the transforming grace of God began to take root and to grow. It has now been more than forty years since I hit anyone, and I hope longer than that since I have scared anyone. My transformation out of self-possessed violence came unexpectedly and permanently. Something that can only be described as glorious happened to me.

One day when I was fifteen I went with three friends to a secret place on campus where we could hide out and smoke. We got into an argument with some other boys who were there. We flashed our knives and thankfully they left. As we finished our cigarettes and walked away the thought that someone could have been killed came to me. Suddenly I was absorbed in wondering what my mother would have thought if I had killed someone.

My thoughts didn't have anything to do with punishment or with my mother being angry. Instead, I thought of all the dreams she had for me, of the kind of man she hoped I would become. I knew without having to put it into words that the menial, hard, backbreaking work she went to in that hospital kitchen every day was an investment in my future. My thoughts all had to do with knowing that I was freely and completely loved with no desire for anything but to be loved in return. That was the last time that I ever carried a weapon.

Then Brenda and I became high-school sweethearts. Brenda abhorred violence. She was quiet, intellectual, gentle. She had a reputation for being naturally friendly and kind to everyone, to both the popular and the outcasts. She did not approve of my fighting, and if there was anything I wanted, it was her approval. Being around her made me feel more tranquil. She introduced me to poetry and to the idea that there might be a depth and meaning to life worth exploring. It was healing to feel loved by her. She is the love of my life.

Eventually I came to see that God was loving me through my mother, through Brenda, and through my older sisters, who gave me such wonderful childhood memories. I saw that the love of God was not an abstraction. God's love is a reality that was with me and had always been with me even in the worst of times. As I reflect on my life I see that, to me, Christ is God saying, "I love you with a love that desires nothing but your good, and nothing can ever separate you from my love."

Love saved my life. Love has given me a life. How, then, can I live in any way other than with gratitude for Love? How can I deny "God is love"? Should I renounce God as the source and strength of everything that is good? How can I not long to live with the compassion, the mercy, and the kindness of Christ?

To abandon love would be unimaginably sad. It would be a complete waste. For me personally it would mean that the great miracle of grace had been lost on me. But that is also what it means for every individual, and for the church, and for our world. The saints have all tried to help us see that the supreme goal of the Christian life, whether contemplated individually or collectively, is to love as God loves, which is to love in a way that requires an essential simplicity and willingness to receive God's love—"to let love happen."[42] We are brought full circle to Neil Diamond's lament:

> The good Lord loves you so
> Ain't it sad we're doing so bad?

· 2 ·

Overcoming Evil with Good

—————◦———

Let love be genuine; hate what is evil, hold fast to what is good; love one another with mutual affection; outdo one another in showing honor. Do not lag in zeal, be ardent in spirit, serve the Lord. Rejoice in hope, be patient in suffering, persevere in prayer. Contribute to the needs of the saints; extend hospitality to strangers.

Bless those who persecute you; bless and do not curse them. Rejoice with those who rejoice, weep with those who weep. Live in harmony with one another; do not be haughty, but associate with the lowly; do not claim to be wiser than you are. Do not repay anyone evil for evil, but take thought for what is noble in the sight of all. If it is possible, so far as it depends on you, live peaceably with all. Beloved, never avenge yourselves, but leave room for the wrath of God; for it is written, "Vengeance is mine, I will repay, says the Lord." No, "if your enemies are hungry, feed them; if they are thirsty, give them something to drink; for by doing this you will heap burning coals on their heads." Do not be overcome by evil, but overcome evil with good.

ROMANS 12:9–21

Recognizing Evil

When M. Scott Peck was writing his book on the nature of evil he asked his then eight-year-old son if he knew what evil was. His son answered immediately: "Sure Dad, evil is live spelled backwards." Peck says that his son was exactly right. Evil is what destroys life in any way—physically, spiritually, intellectually, psychologically, or emotionally.

Peck lists several criteria for detecting evil. Evil as a discreet diagnostic category includes the same abdication of responsibility found in other character or personality disorders, but it is further distinguished by:

1. consistent destructive scapegoating behavior, which may often be quite subtle.
2. excessive, albeit usually covert, intolerance to criticism and other forms of narcissistic injury.
3. pronounced concern with a public image and self-image of respectability, contributing to a stability of life-style but also to pretentiousness and denial of hateful feelings or vengeful motives.
4. intellectual deviousness, with an increased likelihood of a mild schizophreniclike disturbance of thinking at times of stress.[1]

Evil usually has a history. Truly evil people leave a wake of destruction and death, a trail of hurt as they move through life. This is most clearly seen in their behavior toward those who are powerless and vulnerable—the elderly, children, and the poor. A Saddam Hussein or an Idi Amin is not evil because of one or two dark incidents, but because their cruelty is chronic. It is not that the evil person has no feelings of conscience or sense of sin, but that he or she is unwilling to tolerate a painful conscience or knowledge of guilt. The evil suffer from "malignant narcissism," an "unsubmitted will."[2] All mentally healthy individuals submit themselves "to something higher than themselves, be it God or truth or love or some other ideal. . . . Not so the evil, however. In the conflict between their guilt and their will, it is the guilt that must go and the will must win."[3] To refuse to submit to anything other than one's own will automatically means enslavement to the forces of evil.[4] It is extremely important to evil people that they appear as if they are good. For example, a politician may talk plausibly of working to create a "culture of life," but consistently act in such a way as to suppress life. The evil are liars and the lies they tell are meant to create an illusion of honor, decency, and humanity. "They are," says Peck, "unceasingly engaged in the effort to maintain the appearance of moral purity. . . . Evil originates not in the absence of guilt but in the effort to escape it."[5]

Evil people, therefore, engage in unrelenting scapegoating. Whatever is wrong is somebody else's fault. Adolf Hitler rose to power by blaming all of Germany's woes on Jews. To illustrate scapegoating Peck uses this example from ordinary life: A six-year-old boy asks, "Daddy, why did you call Grandma a bitch?" The father shouts, "Now you're going to get it! I'm going to teach you not to use such filthy language!" He drags the boy upstairs to the soap dish. "In the name of proper discipline," says Peck, "evil has been committed."[6] Instead of acknowledging and dealing with their own failures, chronically evil people and societies blame and attack those who are powerless to defend themselves. "Strangely enough," Peck concludes, "evil people are often destructive because they are attempting to destroy evil. The problem is that they misplace the locus of the evil. Instead of destroying others they should be destroying the sickness within themselves. As life often threatens their self-image of perfection, they are often busily engaged in hating and destroying that life—usually in the name of righteousness."[7]

And so Peck titled his book *People of the Lie*. There are not many people, Peck maintains, who are truly evil. Most of us are rather ordinary, garden-variety sinners. We are appropriately ashamed of the wrong things we do and the bad choices we make in life. But hurting others is not the characteristic pattern of our lives. And while we might engage in some blaming of others, we do feel some sense of responsibility and culpability for the troubles of the world. Peck argues that really evil people are, for the most part, not in prisons and jails. Really evil people are most frequently to be found in places like churches and in political office. They are, after all, "people of the lie."[8]

War is a specific evil—an evil used to further other evil ends by self-justifying, self-gratifying, self-promoting governments and leaders. The appearance of goodness in the people who design, declare, and maintain wars is a lie—a lie so commonly told that it takes genuine effort to disbelieve it. While it is important to understand the evil of war, we must also understand the ease with which we choose the same evil. Whether as citizens of a wealthy nation whose prosperity depends on militarism, or as people choosing to oppose war, the evil of violence waits just at our elbow, waiting for us to grasp and unleash it. We must understand this temptation to power and how evils, such as war, are best confronted and overcome.

Three Who Faced Violence

One of the most frequent reasons Christians give for supporting American military intervention all over the world is that they must stand up to evil. It is absolutely correct that Christians must stand up to evil, but not by using military force. It is a maxim of the Christian faith that evil must be courageously exposed and confronted. The question, then, is How are we guided by our faith in the struggle with evil? As we attempt to form an answer to this query it might be helpful to reflect on the responses of three Christians who had to choose how to face evil in its most terrifying forms.

Dietrich Bonhoeffer

Dietrich Bonhoeffer has proven to be one of the most admired and respected pastors and theologians of the twentieth century. Bonhoeffer said that we must not only help the victims of injustice, we must also be willing to throw ourselves into the gears of evil if that is what it takes to stop the machinery itself. It was Bonhoeffer's deep and passionate belief that Christians have no alternative but to fight evil with all of the power that God gives them.

As Hitler rose to power in Germany, Bonhoeffer was stunned, frustrated, and angered by how readily the church consented to and complied with the Nazi regime. Under ever-escalating sanctions, Bonhoeffer spoke and wrote extensively in opposition to Hitler's treatment of Jews and the State's assertion of authority over the church. He helped to create the Confessing Church, which, unlike the official State Church, resisted Hitler's control and the sinister influence of fascism.

Early on, Bonhoeffer was able to find safe havens, first in England and then in the United States, where he could take a stand for Christian justice and goodness. He accepted a professorship at Union Theological Seminary in New York but then resigned almost immediately. If he sat out the bloody conflict at a distance and in safety, he said, he would not possess the necessary integrity to contribute substantially to the restoration of Germany after the war. And so he courageously returned to Nazi Germany—prepared to throw himself into "the machinery of evil" if need required it.[9]

For a while Bonhoeffer ran a secret seminary. Eventually he was sickened by the way in which even the Confessing Church compromised with Hitler. He became heroically involved in clandestine efforts to help Jews escape Europe. He was arrested, and while he was in prison the Gestapo discovered that his involvement in the German resistance movement was far deeper than they had guessed.

Bonhoeffer had been a participant in a failed assassination plot against Hitler. He explained to his sister what compelled him to act so contrarily to his pacifist beliefs: "If I see a madman driving a car into a group of innocent bystanders, then I can't as a Christian simply wait for the catastrophe and then comfort the wounded and bury the dead. I must try to wrestle the steering wheel out of the hands of the driver."[10] After a year and a half in confinement and just days before the Allies liberated the prison, Hitler sent word that Bonhoeffer and his fellow conspirators, who were both family and friends, should not survive the war. On April 9, 1945 the SS at the Flossenburg prison camp hanged Bonhoeffer, who had shown extraordinary calm, kindness, and courage during all the long months of his imprisonment.

Bonhoeffer is so significant to our understanding of Saint Paul's Epistle to the Romans precisely because he was a person of genuine goodness and faith who succumbed to the temptation to overcome evil with evil. I want to be very careful here. What I am saying is obviously and necessarily a rather simplistic portrayal, but I think not inaccurate. Bonhoeffer was a brilliant theologian, and a person of immense spiritual integrity. Over the last forty years his most famous book, *The Cost of Discipleship*, has had a profound impact on my personal spiritual formation. It seems to me, however, that to interpret Bonhoeffer's actions, as many do, as a willingness to give up personal purity in the hope of saving millions of lives, as a willingness to sin for the sake of others, and as an act of surrender to God is overly idealistic, romanticized, and perhaps a little too messianic.

I have no trouble accepting this interpretation as Bonhoeffer's self-understanding, but neither do I doubt that, like the rest of us, Bonhoeffer may not always have understood his own motives with absolute clarity. The smarter one is the more sophisticated his or her rationalizations become. Whenever we decide to take matters into our own hands, whenever we decide that the course of history rests upon our shoulders, whenever we decide that by sinning we can overcome sin, the nature and quality of

our surrender become suspect. Bonhoeffer's greatness is seen
not in the assassination attempt that sent him to prison, but in
the way he embraced the suffering of Christ in prison. I cannot
believe that God was in the attempted violence, that God willed
such a thing or was part of the conspiracy, but in that desperate
place called Flossenburg I see a light that can only be the light
of Christ.

In the end, of course, Bonhoeffer and the others did not succeed in "wresting the steering wheel" from the madman's hands.
Their effort to shorten the war through assassination came to
nothing. All they succeeded in doing was in heightening Hitler's
already lethal paranoia. Over and over again history has shown
that violence is ineffective, that it only adds fuel to violence and
cruelty, thus increasing the weight of the world's already terrible
suffering. What a force for peace, a light for faith and hope and
love, Bonhoeffer would have been in our world if he had only
followed, to the end, and without wavering, his original commitment to costly discipleship, to suffer with his people in such
a way that they would be "able to hear the word of God again."

While suffering suffocating oppression, Bonhoeffer wrote in
The Cost of Discipleship: "From now on there can be no more
wars of faith. The only way to overcome our enemies is by loving them. . . . The will of God is that men should defeat their
enemies by loving them . . . our enemies being those who have
perhaps already raised their hand to kill us. . . . Only one thing
is required—to rely on Christ's word, and cling to it as offering
greater security than all the securities in the world."[11]

Martin Luther King Jr.

Like Bonhoeffer, Martin Luther King Jr. believed that Christians
have a responsibility to stand up to the systemic evil of their
own societies regardless of the personal cost. I use the word
evil because the lynchings, the beatings, and the horrendous oppression of African Americans need to be described by a word

that connotes something far more terrible than the meaning implied by expressions like "violations of civil rights." Too easily we forget what we have done.

Just months after fourteen-year-old Emmett Till was beaten beyond recognition and then shot to death for whistling at a white woman, Rosa Parks was arrested for refusing to get up and give her seat on the bus to a white man. Angry black teenagers began sharpening knives and collecting baseball bats. But African American ministers who already recognized Martin Luther King Jr. as one of their leaders persuaded the teenagers and the black community to move in a more creative and effective direction. They organized a bus boycott. The boycott lasted a year, and it required that the African Americans of Memphis, Tennessee, suffer numerous hardships. Many of these men and women walked miles to work, worked all day, and then walked those miles home again at night. But the black community perpetrated no violence.[12] A better solution had been found. The boycott successfully changed that mean-spirited law, and it generated incredible energy for the just aims of the Civil Rights Movement.

One night a bomb exploded on King's front porch. His wife and young children were in the house; any of them could have been injured or killed. But this is what King said to the crowd that gathered around his family: "If you have weapons, take them home: if you do not have them, please do not seek to get them. . . . We must love our white brothers no matter what they do to us. . . . Jesus still cries out in words that echo across the centuries: 'Love your enemies: bless them that curse you; pray for them that despitefully use you!' This is what we must live by. We must meet hate with love."[13]

Festo Kivengere

Bishop of the Diocese of Kigezi and often called "Africa's Apostle of Love,"[14] Festo Kivengere, was one of the most beautiful

Christians of the twentieth century. He was a humble man from a remote tribe in Uganda who had spent his youth herding his father's cattle. Kivengere was consecrated as the Anglican Bishop of Kigezi in Uganda in 1972, just as Idi Amin's reign of terror was growing even more brutal and intense.

When Amin overthrew Uganda's first prime minister, Milton Obote, in 1971, he immediately began arresting anyone suspected of not supporting him. Hundreds of soldiers from the Lango and Acholi tribes were ruthlessly shot down in their barracks. Amin ordered fifty-five thousand persons, mostly prosperous middle-class merchants from India and Pakistan, expelled from Uganda. A pastor who read a Psalm that mentioned Israel during a radio broadcast was shot for doing so. When husbands and wives set out for work in the morning neither knew whether the other would return home that night. Amin probably tortured and killed five hundred thousand men and women.[15]

Several months before his consecration as bishop, Kivengere gave this response to the growing cruelty and danger faced by Ugandan Christians:

> The cross speaks of life in conflict with death, life defeating death. . . . The cross is . . . God moving in love to meet violent men and women, God facing violence and suffering for us. . . . Your faith was born in violence. The Christian is not scared when nations are upset, when the whole world is shaking. Your faith was born on Calvary—it can stand anything.[16]

Repeatedly risking torture and death, Bishop Kivengere met face to face with Amin to plead for the lives of condemned prisoners. At one point three thousand people in the city of Kabale, where Kivengere and his wife, Mera, lived, were ordered by Amin to come to the stadium to see three men killed. The hearts of the people were filled with fear as a truck drove into the arena and unloaded the three young men in chains. Kivengere turned to two of his pastor friends and said, "I can't just sit here. I'm going to see if I can talk to these three before they are shot." His friends begged him not to. They were afraid that he would either be led away to be tortured or that he would be shot and killed on the spot.

Kivengere walked across the arena and asked for permission to speak to the men. To everyone's astonishment his request was granted. As he approached the three men, he could see, to his surprise, that their faces were entirely peaceful. They thanked him for coming and told him that as Christians they trusted that in spite of death all would be well with them. They asked him for only one thing, that he tell their wives and children that they loved them and to keep on trusting in Christ. Kivengere said, "Why, the people we need to be talking to are the soldiers in the firing squad—not these men."

The soldiers in the firing squad, who had heard most of what the prisoners had said, were in a state of shock. They didn't know what to do. The prisoners smiled at the crowd, raised their chained hands, and waved. People saw the peace of God on their faces, and those who were close enough to hear reported their conversation with Kivengere. Then the shots rang out, and the three men fell dead. A great many people, including some of the soldiers on the firing squad, came to faith that day and enlarged the peaceable kingdom. They wanted what could give such peace and joy in the face of violence and death. That is overcoming evil with good.[17]

Festo Kivengere could do little to prevent the slaughter in Uganda but to proclaim the truth. He preached encouragement to the people. "When we stand where our Lord stood in this world, representing the Light and Truth, we are an embarrassment and a threat to the darkness. We are likely to be hated and called a 'subversive community.'"[18] In another sermon he said, "Some think power is force and guns. But God gives us greater power. It is the power to love. It is the power to forgive our enemies like Jesus loved and forgave his enemies when he was on the cross. Moreover it becomes clear to us through the Scriptures, that resistance is to be that of overcoming evil with good."[19]

One Sunday eight thousand people came from their villages and sat on the grass to hear Bishop Kivengere preach. He spoke reassuringly of the power of the church to endure:

> In his sermon Festo told the people that when he was a boy he herded his parents' cattle on the great expanse of the grasslands. One day the wind caught sparks from a cooking fire in the village and carried them into the long dry grass. Suddenly the plains were ablaze. Everyone was afraid that the grass roofs of the huts would catch fire and the whole village would be destroyed, but the winds blew the fire away from them. Their huts were saved, but the grazing lands were burned to ashes.
>
> "The next day," Festo said, "I went out to look at the grasslands. Everything was burned to the ground. The land looked black and dead." He recalled how he had cried, "Mother, whatever will happen to our cattle now? There's nothing for them to eat. And the ground looks as if it will never grow grass again."
>
> "Wait a bit," he said his mother answered, "The rains will come. Then the grass will grow again, thicker than ever. The plains will turn green, and the cows will eat."
>
> "And as you know," said Festo finishing the story, "she was right."
>
> Festo then encouraged the people by concluding his sermon like this, "Dear brothers and sisters, our church is about to be burned by the fires of hatred. But no fire can destroy the seeds of faith. Those who hate Christians may hurt us. But we will be like the grass that grows again, strong and thick after the fire. The church in Uganda will keep growing, and soon we will be stronger than ever."[20]

After the ouster of Amin, Bishop Kivengere and his wife, Mera, were instrumental in the reconstruction of Uganda. They helped to make food and medicine and doctors available. They built windmills to bring fresh water to the villages. They saw to it that the most vulnerable people, widows and parentless children, were helped—regardless of their tribe or politics or faith. Kivengere was an apostle of love, overcoming evil with good.[21]

The *Anawim:* The Third Way

Because it counters our instincts to fight or flee and the way that those two instincts have been trained by our culture, the journey along "the third way,"[22] which is nothing less than the path taken by Christ, requires enormous courage and creativity, and a brave spiritual imagination. Fear, hatred, and disbelief blunt our imagination and prevent us from seeing what is really needed in the moment, keeping us from responding to crisis and danger with practical, creative solutions.

Jesus does not deny or attempt to evade the unjust suffering and violence of our world. On the contrary Jesus identifies with those who suffer and asserts: "Blessed are the meek [*anawim* in Hebrew] for they will inherit the earth" (Matthew 5:5). With this statement Jesus urges us to follow him along the path of redemptive suffering.

It is quite astonishing that men and women in developing nations who must cope with unimaginable deprivation and often political oppression are not as troubled as affluent Westerners by the question, "If God is good, then how can God allow so much pain and cruelty to run rampant in our world?" Apparently they tend not to ask such questions because in contemplating the agony of the cross they see their God as one who suffers with them. They understand Christ as the one who chose not to flee but to embrace suffering with redemptive arms and to hold it with healing hands.[23] Through embracing this cruciform way they believe that they are at one with Christ.

When Jesus pronounces the blessing of the *anawim* it is not some vague endorsement of humility. Nor is it a sentimental declaration that it is nice to be nice and good to be good. Rather, it is a serious summons for us to follow Christ, the epitome of true meekness, and to become one of the *anawim* ourselves.

Mother Teresa was certainly one of the *anawim*. I love what Malcolm Muggeridge said of her:

> There is a light in this world, a healing spirit more powerful than any darkness we may encounter. We sometimes lose sight of this force when there is suffering, and too much pain. Then suddenly, the Spirit will emerge through the lives of ordinary people who hear a call and answer in extraordinary ways.[24]

We may get so caught up in Mother Teresa as a kind of celebrity saint that we do not remember her as Agnes Bojaxhiu, an ordinary girl from the little country of Albania. Most of us, like her, are ordinary people, but we each have the capacity to hear a call and to answer in extraordinary ways so that the Spirit emerges through the simplicity and humility of our everyday lives.

The literal *anawim*, the "meek," are without money or power or political influence or any of the resources usually considered necessary to make things happen. Instead, they have learned to depend on God alone. As Johannes Metz wrote in his wonderful little book *Poverty of Spirit:*

> To become a man as Christ did is to practice poverty of spirit, to obediently accept our innate poverty as human beings. This acceptance can take place in many of life's circumstances where the very possibility of being human is challenged. . . . There is the poverty of the average person's life who is unnoticed by the world.

In writing about the shape of this spiritual poverty Metz says,

> Jesus was poor in this way. He was no model figure for humanists, no great artist or statesman, no diffident genius. He was a frighteningly simple man, whose only talent was to do good. The one great passion of his life was "the Father." Yet it was precisely in this way that he demonstrated "the wonder of empty hands" (Bernanos), whose radical dependence on God is no different than anyone else's. He has no talent but that of his own heart, no contribution to make except self-abandonment, no consolation save God alone.[25]

Metz says that we possess nothing, not even our selves. Our very existence is provisional; consequently, "we cannot rest in the security of the present."[26]

In the first chapter of 2 Corinthians Saint Paul says, "I want you to know, my friends, that when we were in the province of Asia things were so bad that we felt like we were dying. Things were so bad that we felt like we were being crushed to death. But it all worked out for something good in that we learned to rely totally on God rather than on ourselves" (paraphrase, 1:8–9). To be meek, or poor in spirit, is to trust in God alone.

The *anawim* of the Psalms and the Beatitudes do not pursue power in the ordinary sense. They have no power, yet they are not weak. They are strong. They are strong because they are not clinging or grasping or in bondage to their own blind will. Because they have nothing to prove, nothing to defend, and nothing to hold onto at all costs, and because they seek nothing but the love of God, they are not afraid.

Peter Barton lived an incredibly exciting and adventuresome life as a young man and then, after the age of thirty, became hugely successful in business. But in the prime of his life—happily married, the father of three children, and successful in every way that the world measures—he was diagnosed with terminal stomach cancer. Of his own demise Peter wrote that once he accepted that his cancer would inevitably kill him, that in an important sense he had no future, he was strangely liberated and even inexplicably happy.[27] When we accept our own powerlessness, our own inability to control the people and events in our lives, we are immediately enveloped in an unfathomable mystical power. The attitude of the meek and humble is the attitude of Christ, who let go and emptied himself of everything except for the love of God. Their attitude is the attitude of healthy religion: the awareness that many of the things we fear most in life are very likely to happen to us but if we trust God none of them are anything to fear.[28]

Our fear fuels the engine of anger, which turns the gears of vengeance. Without the fuel of fear the whole mechanism grinds to a halt. Sometimes a marriage becomes just a vicious circle of insanity with each spouse responding in destructive and crazy ways to the craziness of the other. But if either person can step out of the circle of insanity the energy may go out of the whole thing; it will begin to slow down and eventually stop. But it is easy to see where fear and anger lead: Nazi Germany subjects Jews to unimaginable horror and death; Israel in turn oppresses and brutalizes Palestinians (with American knowledge and support), even with massacres such as at the refuge camps of Sabra and Shatila; some Arabs then resort to global terrorism, with the attack on the World Trade Center as their most heinous assault; America responds by defying the rest of the world, fabricating evidence, and attacking Iraq. Matters of cause and effect are certainly more complex than this; nevertheless there is a relationship here that is characterized by fear and anger.

Meanwhile, the *anawim,* those men and women in whom we find this spiritual quality of meekness, are able to be the non-anxious and non-angry presence that has the power to bring healing where there is conflict—to overcome evil with good.

Sometimes this quality is seen in children who enlighten us by doing and saying the most extraordinary things. For example, in 1960 a federal judge ordered the all-white schools in New Orleans to admit African American students. After several delays a black first-grader, Ruby Bridges, entered William T. Frantz School. Each day Ruby went into the school and left it through a howling mob. She was subjected to violent and vile language. Foul names and curses were hurled at her. People shook their fist, and screamed that they were going to kill her. Robert Coles, the now-famous psychiatrist, went to the school, initially out of curiosity, and observed the calm and dignity with which Ruby passed through the mob. He interviewed her teacher, her parents, and finally Ruby herself.

The teacher told Coles that she had seen Ruby talking to the people in the street, but when Coles asked Ruby about it she said that she wasn't talking to them, she was praying for them. Ruby explained that her parents and her minister said that she ought to pray for such people because "they needed praying for." Coles was perplexed, but on one occasion his wife helpfully asked: "What would you do if you were going through a mob like that twice a day?" She constructed this scenario: "What would you do if to get into the Harvard Club in the morning and leave it in the afternoon you had to go through those mobs, and even the police wouldn't protect you?" Coles decided that the first thing he would do in a situation like that was to call the police. "But Ruby couldn't call the police. The police were on the side of the mobs." The second thing he thought he would do was to get a lawyer. "Ruby had no lawyer. Ruby had not even been born at the hands of a doctor." The third thing Coles thought he would attempt would be to use his training, his knowledge, and his skill with language against these people. He would expose their sickness and marginal intelligence. "But Ruby did not have the language of sociology or psychology to turn on this crowd. She would not even call them rednecks." The fourth thing Coles told his wife he might do in Ruby's circumstances would be to write an article about it, maybe even turn it into a book. "But Ruby was just learning to read and write." What Ruby did was to pray for them, not only as she passed through their mindless rage twice a day, but at night before she went to bed. She told Coles that she should especially be the one to pray for them. When he asked why, she said, "Because if you go through what they are doing to you, you're the one who should be praying for them. . . . The minister said that Jesus went through a lot of trouble, and he said about the people who were causing the trouble, 'God forgive them, because they don't know what they're doing.'"[29]

Coles concluded his 1985 article in *Christianity Today,* "The Inexplicable Prayers of Ruby Bridges," this way:

> What does this leave us with now? The great paradox that Christ reminded us about is that sometimes those who are lonely and hurt and vulnerable—*meek,* to use the word—are touched by grace and can show the most extraordinary kind of dignity, and in that sense, inherit not only the next world, but even at times moments of this one. We who have so much knowledge and money and power look on confused, trying to mobilize the intellect to figure things out. It is not so figurable, is it? These things are mysteries. As Flannery O'Connor said, "Mystery is a great embarrassment to the modern mind."[30]

The meek, then, are not self-pitying victims. There is a personal and prayerful dignity and bravery about them.[31] In their humility we see the potent cure for the narcissistic spirit of evil. To say that the meek are not afraid is to say that they have the courage to speak the truth. Jesus bravely challenged the veracity and integrity and the goodness of the political and religious leaders of his day. Jesus referred to Herod as "that fox" (Luke 13:32). He accused the top religious leaders of the most egregious kinds of hypocrisy: exploiting the poor, greed, self-serving crimes, and clever manipulations to make themselves look good when inside they were as rotten as a decaying corpse. When we question whether we should stand up to evil the *anawim* reply gently, but ever so firmly, "Yes, stand up to evil, name it, expose it. Like Ruby Bridges, let your light shine into the shadows and the light will dispel the darkness."

Let your light shine in the darkness like Bishop Festo Kivengere, Martin Luther King Jr., or Sister Dianna Ortiz. On November 2, 1989, Sister Ortiz, an Ursuline nun and U.S. citizen who had gone to Guatemala to teach Mayan children how to read and write, was kidnapped by security forces under the command of an American. She was taken to a secret prison where over the next twenty-four hours she was tortured and raped. The wounds on her back from 110 cigarette burns may have healed by now, but the lacerations to her spirit remain, as do the haunting memories of the cries and screams of the men and women with her in that prison. Sister Ortiz vowed that she would "tell the world" what she saw and heard during that day in the highlands of western Guatemala, that she would make known what she calls her "journey from torture to truth."[32]

The truth is that the United States has long been involved in military coups, torture, and assassinations in Central and South America. The truth is that the United States runs its own school of terrorism, the School of the Americas (now the "Western Hemisphere Institute for Security Cooperation"), which has educated Central and South American military personnel in the use of torture and has trained some of the most sadistic and bloodiest murderers in the world—including those who murdered six prominent Jesuit priests, their housekeeper, and her daughter in Nicaragua in 1989.[33] These infamous killings, it may be remembered, took place at the University of Central America where the priests taught and lived. They appeared to have been tortured and then shot execution style. Some of the victims had chunks of flesh gouged out, and the brains of two lay several feet from the blood-spattered bodies. Noam Chomsky quotes

Ambrose Evans-Pritchard concerning murder and torture in El Salvador: "The army . . . 'learnt its tricks at American counterinsurgency schools in Panama and the United States. 'We learnt from you', a death squad member once told an American reporter, 'we learnt from you the methods, like blowtorches in the armpits, shots in the balls.'" Chomsky continues,

> The careful observer will find that the worst atrocities have regularly been conducted by elite battalions fresh from their U.S. training. Salvadoran officers who admit their participation in death squad killings describe their service under CIA control and their training sessions on effective torture conducted by U.S. instructors. . . . The bare statistics do not convey the true picture. The true picture in El Salvador is given by the skulls and skeletons in the "body dump" at El Playón, or the scene of women hanging from their feet, their breasts cut off and facial skin peeled back, bleeding to death after the army has passed through.[34]

Like Sister Ortiz and little Ruby Bridges, however, the *anawim* harm no one. Although they do not have the power to protect even themselves, they nevertheless have the courage to pray for their enemies and to speak the simple truth even if the truth is that the world's one superpower is malevolently present when innocent men and women—even citizens of that same superpower—are raped and tortured in a chamber of horrors. In the short run the qualities of faith and love and truth may seem no match for brute force, but in time they are unbelievably powerful. William James said, "I am for those tiny invisible molecular forces that work from individual to individual, creeping through the crannies of the world like so many soft rootlets, or like the capillary oozing of water, but which, given time, will rend the hardest monuments of men's pride."[35] This is the way of good overcoming evil.

In the Heart

While traveling in India, Joseph Stalin's daughter, Svetlana, read Chester Bowles's *Ambassador's Report* and was mesmerized by these words: "It is possible for a single individual to defy the whole might of an unjust empire to save his honor, his religion, his soul, and lay the foundation for that empire's fall or its regeneration." Svetlana called a taxi and was driven to the American embassy, where she asked for asylum.[36] What Bowles's words say to me is that good is ultimately stronger than evil and that you and I can, through humility and faith, play a creative and significant role in the redemptive work of God.

The triumph of good over evil is something that must take place in my own heart, just as it first took place in the heart of Jesus—in the heart of Jesus facing temptation in the desert, in the heart of Jesus tested in Gethsemane, in the heart of Jesus hanging in agony and loving forgiveness on the cross. Having gone ahead of us, Jesus has marked the path we must follow. It is the path of meekness, willingness, self-surrender, openness, receptivity, and faith as ultimate trust. According to Gerald May, "God's love for the person and the person's love for God form a bedrock upon which serious practical efforts can be made to promote good and lessen evil."[37] May goes on to say that evil constitutes an attack upon one's initial surrender and after failing at that, it attempts to weaken the strength and completeness of ongoing surrender. But, May asserts, it is only by reaffirming one's surrender that "truly loving and compassionate service in the world" is possible.[38]

The meek simply do what needs doing without being overly invested in the outcome or in trying to force things to turn out exactly as they want. They are not serious in such a way that their seriousness becomes part of the problem. Like Jesus they can view some of the crazy ironies of human behavior with a certain amount of humor. There is some relaxation, at times even playfulness, in their efforts. The great Chinese teacher Lao Tsu said, "The sage seems to work without doing."[39] The meek feed the hungry because that is what needs doing, not because of "any self-serving *holy* motive."[40]

Similarly, they promote peace, resist injustice, and denounce cruelty wherever these exist without the need for recognition. May asserts that this "same kind of approach applies in resisting or countering any manifestation of evil in the world, be it oppression, pestilence, genocide, or whatever form it may take. . . . But if one allows the complexities of the action to eclipse the simple willingness of one's soul toward God, narcissism will creep in. Then it will be all too easy to contribute to the bloodshed in the name of trying to stop it or to accentuate hatred in the name of love."[41] Ultimately the only way for the church, and the individual men and women who constitute the Body of Christ, to overcome evil and violence is by becoming one with Christ through self-emptying love—not by the exercise of worldly power and force.

What we are talking about is not just our attitude toward war and peace, or a concept about how to meet the assault of evil on our world. What we are really talking about is the spiritual life. What should be obvious, even to those of us who are novices in this regard, is that "spirituality is not an aspect of the Christian life; it is the Christian life."[42] It is our way of being in the world. And it is a way of being that can only come about when God is the center of our lives. The spiritual life is one that has been consecrated to God—offered, in its entirety, to God. As Norvene Vest observes, "Such offering or consecration does not mean that I withdraw from the world, but, rather, that I recognize God's effective power in me and in the world in the midst of things as I find them."[43] Saint Paul wrote, "It is no longer I who live, but it is Christ who lives in me" (Galatians 2:20). Our way of being, then, is being in Christ, which is the way of loving reconciliation, justice, and peace. The Catechism in the *Book of Common Prayer* offers this instruction, "The mission of the Church is to restore all people to unity with God and each other in Christ."[44] If my heart is consecrated to God then this will be the purpose of my existence, and this purpose will shape my way of being. This way of being, although it appears weak to the world, is full of power: that power—that goodness—that overcomes evil.

America and the Holy War Myth

———————————

I am distressed, O Lord,
  by the attitudes and actions of those
    who claim to honor Your name
      and to live within Your purposes.

They don't really listen to Your Word.
They appear to be following some other god
  or are simply taking the path
    of least resistance.
They assume that their wishes are Your will,
  that the crowd they travel with
  or the nations that govern them
    are righteously carrying out Your objectives
      irrespective of their ungodly
      means and methods.

How long, O Lord, must I dwell
  in a world that breeds violence
  and amongst people that engage in war?

Teach me, O God, how to be a peacemaker,
  how to confront violence with love,
  how to courageously and patiently promote
    Your will and Your Word
      among the hostile and angry masses.

PSALM 120, *PSALMS NOW*, BY LESLIE F. BRANDT

War and Scripture

A war-weary Abraham Lincoln noted that both sides in the American Civil War had prayed for God's blessing but that God had not fully answered the prayers of either.[1] It seems never really to have occurred to either the North or the South that perhaps their prayers had not been answered because war is itself evil, and that God does not bless the carnage that human beings inflict on one another in battle. In spite of the fact that this terrible conflict was rooted more in economics than in great moral principles,[2] both sides firmly believed that their cause was just and their aims holy.

I do not suppose that any nation has ever gone to war without believing in the rightness of doing so. The men and women of both the Confederacy and the Union were part of a culture that emphasized the importance of the Bible and church attendance. Many of these people and their clergy believed in the holy war tradition of the Old Testament, as represented in stories like that of Gideon, who was called by God to deliver Israel from Midianite oppression. The Confederates and Unionists both believed they had biblical warrant for killing and maiming and burning one another. "Mine eyes have seen the glory of the coming of the Lord," they sang, "he is trampling out the vintage where the grapes of wrath are stored."

That the Old Testament Scriptures contain a holy war tradition is obvious; less clear is how to handle such texts. For example, it is difficult to know in every case whether the decision to go to war was truly the will of God, or whether God's name was invoked as a cover for human will and aggression—just as the providence of God was repeatedly appealed to in America's invasion of Iraq.[3] The late Joseph Swaim, pastor and professor of biblical exegesis, noted that "under the monarchy, war became for Israel an instrument of national policy, the king declaring it at will."[4]

Dale Brown has suggested that the holy wars of Hebrew

Scriptures are to be understood as miracle stories.[5] Decisive victories against incredible odds were meant to teach the people to rely on God rather than on their own military strength. If the entire Old Testament story of Gideon is read in this light, which seems to be the obvious way to read it, then there is very little support to be found for trusting in nuclear arsenals, military technology that shocks and terrorizes, unproven trillion-dollar defense shields, or for relying on a superpower status that will never end.

It is also possible that the holy war tradition in Scripture is to be understood as a concession by God, so that the holy wars represent not God's original intention but a kind of divine concession.[6] When the people of Israel demand a king, God warns them that if they choose a king an oppressive military-commercial complex will dominate their lives. Samuel warns:

> "These will be the ways of the king who will reign over you: he will take your sons to . . . be his horsemen . . . to plow his ground and to reap his harvest . . . He will take your daughters to be perfumers and cooks . . . He will take the best of your fields and vineyards . . . and give them to his officers and courtiers. . . . He will take . . . the best of your cattle . . . He will take one-tenth of your flocks, and you shall be his slaves." (1 Samuel 8:7–22)

But they respond, in effect, that they don't care. They want a king. They have thought about it and they know best. They insist on rejecting God as their only king and choose Saul to govern them. God concedes (1 Samuel 8:22).

God's concession to the people of Israel, allowing them kings who would make war, is not indicative of the life of Jesus, or the standard by which Jesus' followers lived. In the Gospels Jesus insists that where there is a discrepancy between a concession and God's original plan, it is the primordial divine intention and not the concession that should be our chief guide. The spiritual life is characterized by a warm and softhearted willingness rather than by hardhearted willfulness. Christians themselves have been fond of quoting the words of the prophet Ezekiel: "Thus says the Lord God,. . . . A new heart I will give you, and a new spirit I will put within you; and I will remove from your body the heart of stone and give you a heart of flesh" (Ezekiel 36:22, 26). It is the will of God, not God's concession, to which we seek to be most attentive and receptive—the rule of God, and not of militaristic kings or ambitious politicians.

In the end the primary exegetical principle to be followed by those within the Christian tradition is that the Old Testament must be interpreted in the light of the New Testament, and both the Old and New Testaments must be interpreted in the light of our knowledge of the mind of Christ.[7] Apart from our having the mind of Christ in us, apart from humility and love, we can know nothing. Understanding is not brought about by meticulously combing through Scripture to find a proof text supporting our preconceived notions; it comes from trusting Christ and consecrating our hearts to the way of Christ. It is not the holy war stories of the Old Testament that are most helpful in coming to know the mind of God, but in identifying with the reality of the Hebrew concepts of *hesed,* which is patient, tenacious, loving-kindness, and *shalom,* which is peace characterized by integrity, community, wholeness, justice, and harmony. These are the qualities that can lead us to true understanding. *Hesed* and *shalom* are the mind of Christ.

The single word that most characterized the passion and wisdom of the ancient prophets in regard to all matters, and which is the most essential to understanding their writings, is *justice.* Their emphasis was not on an external code of justice, but the God whose being is expressed in justice—a justice infused with the mystery of God. "Clouds and thick darkness are round about God; righteousness and justice are the foundations of God's throne" (Psalm 97:2). For the prophets, worship of God apart from the practice of justice is impotent and without substance. Where there is no respect for justice fire is uselessly kindled on the altar (Malachi 1:10; 2:17). The great Jewish scholar and mystic Abraham Heschel said that the fundamental meaning of justice "refers to all actions which contribute to maintaining the covenant, namely the true relationship between persons and between the individual and God."[8] According to Heschel, "Justice is not an ancient custom, a human convention, a value, but a transcendent demand, freighted with divine concern. It is not only a relationship between man and man, it is an act involving God, a divine need."[9] Injustice is wrong not because it violates a law in some book but because it hurts people and contradicts the inherent goodness of God. "You shall not abuse any widow or orphan. If you do abuse them, when they cry out to me, I will surely hear their cry . . . for I am compassionate" (Exodus 22:22–23, 27). To be a spiritual or just person in the eyes of the prophets is to be one who has identified with the concerns and character of God and the hurts and needs of humanity. "Seek justice, rescue the oppressed, defend the orphan, plead for the widow" (Isaiah 1:17).

Joseph Swaim, in *War, Peace, and the Bible*, comments on the prophets and their understanding of war and justice like this: "It was clear from the beginning that war could never bring about the society God intended. . . . Better times will come only when they 'speak the truth to one another, render . . . judgments that are true and make for peace, do not devise evil in their hearts' (Zechariah 8:16ff.); 'my servant, says the Lord . . . will bring forth justice to the nations' (Isaiah 42:1)."[10] Only having the mind in us that was in Christ Jesus can bring about the society God intended (Philippians 2:1–5). The point I am making about justice is similar to what Alfred, Lord Tennyson was saying in "Flower in the Crannied Wall":

Flower in the crannied wall,
I pluck you out of the crannies;
I hold you here, root and all, in my hand,

Little flower—but *if* I could understand
What you are, root and all, and all in all,
I should know what God and man is.[11]

If we could understand what justice, *hesed*, and *shalom* are, "root and all, and all in all," we would understand war in the context of both the Hebrew and Christian Scriptures, and we would "know what God and humankind is."

Just War Theory

There is a story told in 2 Chronicles 28 that is relevant to our reflection. In this story the Samaritans had defeated the people of Judah with "a great slaughter." They took thousands of women and children captive, and they plundered Judah. Oded, a little-known Hebrew prophet, said that the army had brought guilt upon Samaria. "You have," he said to the army, "killed them in a rage that has reached up to heaven" (2 Chronicles 28:9). Judah had done wrong, Oded declared, but so had Samaria. Then following the earlier paradigm of Elisha (2 Kings 6:11–23), the Samaritans returned the looted property to the captives and took the captives home. They clothed the prisoners, gave them sandals, provided them with food and water, and carried those too weak to walk back to Jericho on their own donkeys. This is justice. Perhaps in reflecting on stories like this and on the holy war tradition of the Old Testament, and certainly in hopes of constraining some of the sheer horror of war, Christian thinkers beginning with Saint Augustine have developed certain criteria for waging what they have called a "just war."

The first and most essential requirement for a war to be just is that it has a just cause. A just war must be waged for an honorable reason. There are other requirements; for example, it must be pursued according to just means. But the first and most essential requirement is that of a just and honorable cause. This criterion of right intention has come to mean that a just war is fought only as a last resort and in self-defense. There can be no hint of expansionist desires, of greed for what belongs to another nation, of vengeance, or of national, religious, or racial hatred. According to just war theory, a just war is a war of last resort in that once one has been attacked there is no alternative left other than self-defense.

In general Americans believe themselves to be a peaceful and fair people who are willing to live and let live. They imagine themselves to be a people who have gone to war only when necessary to protect their families, or to defend their freedom, or to stop some evil tyrant bent on world domination. Americans like to think of themselves as being very much like the heroes in J. R. R. Tolkien's *Lord of the Rings* trilogy. That they might be the aggressor, heartless and ruthless, is, for most Americans, beyond consideration. But I want to think for a moment about this purity of intention required for a just war—this holiness of motive—in light of American history.

When I was a young boy I thought that my brother, who is six years older than I am, was the world's most admirable person. I thought he could do anything, and he seemed to know everything. When he told me that the United States had never started a war, but always waited until it was attacked first, I believed him completely. Even though I was just a child I felt proud, as I think my brother did, to be part of such a noble country. But I have always loved the study of history—personal and family history, American and world history, and the history of human civilizations. And it was not too many years before I discovered, to my sad disappointment, that America did not possess quite the nobility of character or purity of soul that had so inspired my imagination as a boy. In fact, what I discovered was a long history of wars based on greed, lies, and manipulation of public opinion.

Our March to Empire:
The Sixteenth through Nineteenth Centuries

Leaders of the United States have, throughout this nation's history, used the notion of right intention to justify their aggressive and often bloody actions. In 1829 the newly elected Andrew Jackson, known among Native Americans as Sharp Knife, took office as president of the United States. Jackson and his soldiers had killed thousands of Cherokees, Chickasaws, Choctaws, Creeks, and Seminoles. Nevertheless these people held tightly to their tribal lands, which had been "granted" to them by treaty with the U.S. government. As a solution to this "Indian problem" Jackson proposed in his very first message to Congress that the people of all these tribes be moved west of the Mississippi River. This territory would be "guaranteed to the Indian tribes, as long as they shall occupy it." Initially, the plan was to move the Cherokees in stages because of their large numbers. The discovery of Appalachian gold, however, created a demand for their immediate forced removal. In the fall of 1838 General Winfield Scott herded the Cherokees into stockades—concentration camps. From these prison camps they began a long winter's trek west to Indian Territory. On this death march, known as the "Trail of Tears," one of every four Cherokees died from cold, hunger, or disease.[12]

From the time of Columbus, who described the Taino people of El Salvador Island as "tractable and peaceable," the indigenous peoples of this hemisphere have been enslaved, tortured, and murdered. Their cultures have been destroyed.[13] From the time of the first American colonies the Europeans engaged in genocidal aggression against the Native American population, sometimes using germ warfare by giving them blankets infected with smallpox.[14] This was all "necessary"—justifiable, it was argued—because Native Americans stood in the way of progress and were a threat to American settlers. No one was so crude as to say that it was because they wanted to get rich growing cotton on Native American land, or to ravish Appalachia for its gold. The citizenry of the U.S. did not want to face the truth of these unjust wars then, and it does not want to face the truth now. Although our treatment of the Native American population today remains immoral, demeaning, and oppressive, most Americans dismiss the countless massacres of Native American men, women, and children and all the injustices they have suffered as an aberration in our remote history. But it is not an aberration. It is part of the pattern of American character and values that continues to this day.

The twentieth-century monk Thomas Merton wrote the following passage, which furnishes both a timely and historic perspective on the American concept of peace:

> To some peace merely means the liberty to exploit other people without fear of retaliation or interference. To some peace means the freedom to rob others without interruption. To still others it means the leisure to devour the goods of the earth without being compelled to interrupt their pleasures to feed those whom their greed is starving. And to practically everybody peace simply means the absence of any physical violence that might cast a shadow over their animal appetites for comfort and pleasure.[15]

It is absurd, as Merton goes on to point out, to hope for that peace which is the grace of heaven when our thoughts of peace are "fictions" and "illusions." Yet, America has always had these rather warped values when it comes to peace, and has chased the wind in pursuing empire, in following its avarice, and in succumbing to the temptation of self-justification.

Ironically, while America was busy trying to exterminate the Native American population, it was busy importing Africans who had been stolen from their families, terrorized, stacked like cords of wood on boats, shipped to a frighteningly strange land, and made to live at the mercy of people who denied that they were even human. After their emancipation white America continued to brutalize, beat, lynch, and shoot them, to deny them any way out of poverty, education, a seat at the lunch counter, and a drink of water at the drinking fountain. This too defines what it means to be an American. Our history is simply not the history of a just and noble people who resort to violence only as a last resort to protect life and liberty.

Patrick Henry's famous line "Give me liberty or give me death" is wonderfully passionate. But Patrick Henry was not suffering any great oppression. The real leaders of the American Revolution, for the most part, were wealthy and well-educated landowners and slaveholders who themselves possessed considerable personal liberty. Probably over two-thirds of the American population at that time was not interested in breaking away from England. But these prosperous and powerful people wanted an adjustment in the economic system so that they could make even more money. Taxation without adequate representation may have been a vexing problem for the wealthy colonists, but that did not constitute justification for their violence.

In the nineteenth century the U.S. government, press, and general population were obsessed with rapidly expanding the country. Those of Western European decent, they believed, were born to rule the entire continent. They were of a higher order of humanity, and therefore entitled and obligated to rule over the lands, forests, and mineral wealth from sea to shining sea—even if they had to exterminate the indigenous population or violently rob other governments. In 1845 an editor by the name of John L. O'Sullivan called this obsession "Manifest Destiny." O'Sullivan said, "It is the right of our Manifest Destiny to over spread and to possess the whole of that which Providence has given us for the development of the great experiment of liberty and federative government. It is right such as that of the tree to the space of air and the space for the full expansion of its principle of growth."[16] O'Sullivan was wildly successful in picturing a shameless landgrab as justified by God, by some benevolent destiny, by right, by liberty, and by the very workings of the natural order.

Once consciously embraced and embedded in the imagination of the people, the doctrine of Manifest Destiny was used to justify war with Mexico in 1848. The Texas Revolution had finally been somewhat resolved by 1844. Both Texas and Mexico were to retain the territory they occupied at the time. Mexico agreed that it would recognize Texas if Texas would remain independent. Texas, however, wanted to be annexed by the United States. This issue, along with other questions of expansionism, was central in the political campaign that elected James Polk to the presidency. Polk directed U.S. troops into disputed territory. When there was finally an armed confrontation Polk declared, "A state of war now exists, not withstanding all our efforts to avoid it."[17] Mexico had been successfully provoked and would be decisively defeated. All of America's "high mindedness" was rewarded with the addition of not only Texas, which had already been taken, but also New Mexico, Arizona, Nevada, Utah, and California. By military conquest America seized the entire northern half of Mexico.

Early in 1898 Fitzhugh Lee, American Consul in Cuba, summoned the battleship *Maine* to Havana Harbor to "protect American interests." At first that sounds like something that might have merit, that might meet the standards of a just war. But the expression "American interests" meant then what it means now—using the United States military to ensure the financial profit of big business. This is a long-standing tradition of the United States that runs completely contrary to the just war principle of right or honorable intention. Cuba was still under Spanish rule, but a rebellion, supported by the U.S. government, was under way and was supposedly threatening "American interests." The general Cuban population saw the *Maine* itself as a floating American fortress in their city. They saw it for what it was—an act of aggression. There was an explosion and the

Maine was sunk. No one has ever known for certain who was responsible for the sinking of the *Maine*—Spain, the rebels, an accident, or the U.S. But the American press went all out to blame Spain. The powerful publisher William Randolph Hearst sent Frederick Remington to Cuba to report on the war. Remington contacted Hearst, saying, "There is no war. Request to be called." Hearst responded, "Please remain. You furnish the pictures. I'll furnish the war."[18] The press accused Spain of every imaginable atrocity and evil in Cuba, including cannibalism.[19] Excitement was high in America, for with the defeat of Spain, the U.S. would assume its rightful place as a world power. In this, the Spanish-American War, the United States acquired Puerto Rico, Guam, and the Philippines, but not Cuba. Spain wanted the Americans to annex Cuba and take over Cuba's $400 million debt, but the United States, understanding the business of war very well, refused.[20] It was a different matter with the Philippines. The Port of Manila was ideal for commercial shipping and as a naval base from which America could extend its influence into Asia. The logical conclusion is that the United States wanted a war with Spain out of expansionist desires. It was not a war of last resort or for the sole purpose of self-defense.

At the time of the Spanish-American War there was a rebellion in the Philippines, as there had been in Cuba, against Spanish rule. But in acquiring the Philippines from Spain, the United States determined that the Filipino people were too uncivilized to govern themselves and should, therefore, be brought completely under U.S. military rule. For three years the Filipinos courageously fought for their freedom. It is estimated that three hundred thousand to one million Filipinos died fighting for their independence from the American forces, who used torture in interrogation and applied the same barbaric tactics that had been found to be so successful against the indigenous peoples of the continental United States.[21] Former president Benjamin Harrison urged the annexing of Spain itself, and politicians and journals spoke of extending the "empire."[22] But an eager leap to war and heinous acts of violence cannot be justified by such dubious doctrines as "Manifest Destiny."

All the Explanations in the World:
The Twentieth and Twenty-First Centuries

World War I began for the United States with the sinking of a passenger ship, the *Lusitania,* by a German submarine off the coast of Scotland in 1915. The Germans were attempting to blockade England. The British found a way to get through the blockade by secretly transporting munitions manufactured in the United States on passenger ships. Germany gave extensive notice to the U.S. government and to the public that it would begin sinking passenger ships suspected of transporting arms. Many U.S. citizens sailed on the *Lusitania* in spite of the warning. The ship sank only twenty minutes after being hit, and it has long been held that it went down so quickly because it did in fact carry a large cargo of artillery shells and millions of rounds of small arms ammunition.[23]

The sinking of the *Lusitania* appears to be more of an excuse than a principled justification for entering World War I against the Germans. The United States, by becoming an arms supplier to Great Britain, had in truth entered the war on the side of the French and British before the sinking of the *Lusitania* took place. This was even more true of World War II, considering the Lend-Lease Act of 1941,[24] which authorized the president to transfer arms, without payment, to any government whose defense the president thought vital to the defense of the United States. Senator Robert Taft, and others, argued that the Lend-Lease Act brought the United States one step closer to the conflict in Europe by allowing the president to carry on a kind of undeclared war all over the world.[25]

In terms of just war theory World War II meets the criterion of right motive more than any other war the U.S. has engaged in. However, the traditional peace churches—the Mennonites,

Quakers, and Church of the Brethren—raise the critical question: Would Hitler ever have risen to power if the United States had not helped to create the conditions for World War II by playing the decisive role in the humiliating and economically devastating defeat of Germany in World War I?

While one can argue that World War II may have been fought with the right intention, it was certainly not fought with just means. We must consider, for example, the firebombings of Dresden and Tokyo. In the last months of the war the firebombing of Japan's wooden cities resulted in the horrific slaughter of an estimated five hundred thousand people, and left eight million homeless.[26] In the documentary *Fog of War* former Secretary of Defense Robert McNamara acknowledges that he and General Curtis LeMay, the "genius" behind firebombing, were, in all honesty, guilty of war crimes for what they did, but since they were on the winning side there were no consequences to worry about. But if a nation is truly fighting a just war, it will have no war criminals—at least not of this magnitude.

The United States of America has a long and grisly history of savagely attacking and oppressing others—sometimes directly, sometimes indirectly, and sometimes by proxy. In its more recent and nefarious past, it has even overthrown democratically elected governments in Chile and Guatemala.[27]

In early 1970 Salvador Allende was elected president of Chile in spite of massive efforts by the United States to disrupt the election and prevent Allende from becoming president. In the 1964 election the U.S. spent more money per capita to get the Chilean candidate it favored elected than Lyndon B. Johnson and Barry Goldwater spent in their campaigns for the White House.[28] On the political continuum Allende could be described as a European-style social democrat. He sought to nationalize certain major industries, began a free milk program for half a million malnourished children, and advocated a policy of international independence—meaning that Chile would determine what was in its own best interest rather than kowtowing to the dictates of the U.S. government.[29] ITT and PepsiCo, along with mining companies in which Americans were heavily invested, were among the industries Allende wanted to nationalize. They took their complaint directly to President Richard Nixon.[30] With Secretary of State Henry Kissinger, Nixon fretted that successful economic development in Chile—from which the general population benefited rather than large private corporations—would be "contagious." It might, for example, infect Italy and lead to the establishment of some sort of bond between the communists and social democrats, who would then be able to present a unified front. The U.S., then, based its policy on the bizarre notion that "the thing to be feared is a positive example."[31] The U.S. set out to destroy, or, in Nixon's words, "to make the economy of Chile scream."[32] The U.S. ambassador to Chile, Edward Korry, said that the idea was "to do all in our power to condemn Chile and the Chileans to utmost deprivation and poverty."[33] The CIA planted stories and incited labor unrest and strikes. In September 1973 the government fell. Thousands of men and women were arrested, imprisoned, tortured, and murdered. When Korry, as the American ambassador to Chile, spoke to Kissinger of the wanton brutality and torture, Kissinger evidently responded by saying something to the effect that he didn't want to hear any political science lectures. Specifically, he is reported to have said, "We don't care about torture—we care about important things."[34] After Allende's overthrow in the American-backed coup, U.S. economic aid began to flow into the country once more, and the American government gave its generous support to the cruel and murderous dictatorship of Augusto Pinochet.[35]

In Guatemala Jacobo Arbenz Guzman was democratically elected as president in 1951. For ten years Guatemala was one of the most promising democracies in Central and South America. Guzman was a "leftist," but it is generally agreed that he was certainly not a communist. But when he expropriated unused portions of land controlled by American-owned United

Fruit Company (paying the declared tax value) and began to distribute it among landless peasants, he was declared a dangerous communist by President Dwight D. Eisenhower.[36] United Fruit Company controlled 42 percent of the land in Guatemala. It also controlled the International Railway of Central America and Express Electra, the other two major enterprises in Guatemala.[37] The Dulles brothers—John Foster Dulles, Secretary of State, and Allen Dulles, Director of the CIA under Eisenhower—were major stockholders in the company. Eisenhower gave approval for the CIA to stage a coup, and Guatemala's "ten years of spring," as the Guatemalans fondly called it, was over.[38] The new regime of Colonel Castillo Armas was provided with a list of opponents to be eliminated, and the slaughter began. The continuing U.S.-backed effort to eliminate dissidents has resulted in at least one hundred forty-five thousand deaths and the disappearance of another forty-five thousand.[39]

Admittedly, these two events occurred some time ago, but what they demonstrate is a pattern of exploitation, violence, and injustice perpetrated by a nation that boasts of its innocence and goodness. These events mock the claim of America that its wars are just and its motives pure. The pattern is visible everywhere we look. It would be difficult to name a country that has overthrown more democratically elected governments than the United States of America. David Batstone, writing in the progressive Christian journal *Sojourners,* notes that *Newsweek* magazine has recently claimed that some Pentagon insiders, frustrated by the growing quagmire in Iraq, are pushing a plan they have code-named "The Salvador Option." The name alludes to the support of the Reagan administration for the El Salvador death squads in the 1980s. Batstone writes, "How chilling that the Pentagon is seriously considering a plan to take us back to the dark days."[40] But Batstone misses the point. What is chilling is not that this thinking takes us back to a dark place, but rather it is a continuation of the thinking that perpetuates the darkness. These are not the actions of a nation committed to the ethics of just war theory. They are the actions of people in the throes of insatiable greed and narcissism.

Arundhati Roy, in her passionate and eloquent book *War Talk,* says:

> Since the Second World War, the United States has been at war or has attacked, among other countries, Korea, Guatemala, Cuba, Laos, Vietnam, Cambodia, Grenada, Libya, El Salvador, Nicaragua, Panama, Iraq, Somalia, Sudan, Yugoslavia, and Afghanistan. This list should also include the U.S. government's covert operations in Africa, Asia, and Latin America, the coups it has engineered, and the dictators it has armed and supported. It should include Israel's U.S. backed war on Lebanon, in which thousands were killed. It should include the key role America has played in the conflict in the Middle East, in which thousands have died fighting Israel's illegal occupation of Palestinian territory. It should include America's role in the civil war in Afghanistan in the 1980s, in which more than one million people were killed. It should include the embargos and sanctions that have led directly and indirectly to the death of hundreds of thousands of people, most visibly in Iraq. Put it all together and it sounds very much as though there has been a World War III, and that the U.S. government was (or is) one of its chief protagonists.[41]

The history of America is simply not the history of a peaceful nation, but of a nation with a well-established pattern of aggression and a character shaped by repeated violence against its neighbors—violent aggression that is justified by the use of fabrications, and pandering to the fear and greed of the American people. "As a rule," said Abraham Heschel, "those who know how to exploit are endowed with the skill to justify their acts, while those who are easily exploited possess no skill in pleading their own cause."[42] The privileged class in America knows that most people don't want to send their children to die in an aggressive war to increase the wealth of the wealthy, and so they appeal to what is good and honorable in people and to the principles of just war theory. If you want to pay United Fruit Company for land it is not using in order to provide starving people with some means of subsisting, then they claim you are an evil communist. The wealthy and powerful don't talk about the greed of United Fruit Company, or ITT, or oil corporations, but about fighting to keep America "free." They don't talk about going to war for profit. That is anathema to the principles of just war theory. Instead they talk about the need to defend our liberty. Brazilian bishop Dom Helder Camara, using his own experience, describes the situation perfectly: "When I gave food to the poor, they called me a saint; but when I asked why people are poor, they called me a communist."[43]

The reality of our propensity for corporate evil is visible in our self-righteousness and in our deceptiveness. Over and over, war is justified on the basis of false evidence. On July 30 and 31, 1964, an American destroyer, the *Maddox*, was on a reconnaissance mission in North Vietnam's Gulf of Tonkin. South Vietnamese boats from Danang had been shelling North Vietnam. When the *Maddox* came close to the Vietnamese offshore island of Hon Me, three North Vietnamese patrol boats came out. There was a skirmish in which one machine gun bullet struck the destroyer and one of the patrol boats was destroyed. On August 3 and 4 the *Maddox*, along with another destroyer, the *Turner*, returned to the area, which was still being shelled by the South Vietnamese. The *Turner* reported that it had picked up patrol boats approaching at high speed, and the two destroyers fired into the Gulf for much of the night. It was an awesome display of American firepower, but what is now public knowledge is that they were firing at nothing. There simply were no attacking North Vietnamese boats. If there had been they would have been doing nothing more than defending their own waters and their own shores. Nevertheless, President Lyndon Johnson used this incident, or perhaps it would be better to say nonincident, to convince Congress to authorize him to use "all necessary measures to deal with aggression in Vietnam"—an ironic request, in that the aggressor was the United States.[44]

When Iraq invaded Kuwait in 1990, Kuwait paid several public relations firms millions of dollars to bring the world's sympathy to its side.[45] Some of the most inflammatory pieces of evidence to support U.S. military intervention were colossal lies. For example, widely publicized testimony given before the United States Congress asserted that Iraqi soldiers were murdering babies, that they killed Kuwaiti infants by tearing them from their incubators.[46] Aerial photos purporting to show that Saudi Arabia itself was in imminent danger were doctored by the first Bush administration.[47] Had these accusations been true we might have claimed that our use of military force was a humanitarian intervention, which is certainly a consideration in determining right intention in just war theory. That they were deliberate deceptions, however, exposes the centrality of money and power in our motives.

The second invasion of Iraq, under George W. Bush, was predicated on lies that cynically played on both the fears and the humanitarian concerns of the American people. We were told that we were in "imminent danger" of a nuclear attack, and that Iraq was capable of killing thousands of Americans by releasing biological or chemical agents in the continental U.S. It is now obvious that this was a creative fiction used to stir the frenzy for war and to secure votes for the Republican Party. In fact, this strategy of duplicity was so successful that the Democrats, awed by the polls, failed to ask the hard questions that a responsible opposition party ought to be expected to ask. Why, for example, didn't people like Senator John Kerry demand to see credible evidence before giving their assent to the war? If the Democrats were misled it is because they were willingly misled. In the end we went to war in Iraq not because it was just, but because it was politically expedient for career politicians.

Building a Kingdom

In spite of its use of euphemisms and important-sounding catch phrases, the United States of America has always been propelled by imperial ambitions. In *Resurrecting Empire* Rashid Khalidi asserts that it is thirst for empire that drives American policy in the Middle East:

> Some of those in the war party surrounding President Bush, Cheney, and Rumsfeld have been advocating this perilous adventure in Iraq for a long time, and their allies in the media and the think tanks have not hesitated to bandy about words like empire to describe what they are launching. The hubris involved is not unprecedented (even if the global reach and power of the United States is).[48]

What Khalidi writes is certainly consistent with the overall pattern of American history, and exposes the current use of just war theory as self-delusional mythology. We can be sure that this just war myth is not a harmless bit of fiction; for no matter how we rationalize it, following in the footsteps of other fallen Western empires will inevitably prove injurious to both the outward welfare of the nation and to the inner spiritual character of its people. Our sins are always at the same time personal, corporate, and cosmic in their dimensions. A thousand times a day we choose to either think and act lovingly or unlovingly, and each decision is weighted with enormous consequences for our communion with God. Those of us who believe in biblical judgment—some sort of ultimate assessment of our lives—cannot escape how we help or harm all others as the

basis of that judgment. We are all accomplices in the degrada-
tion of our world and of our own souls. The Gospel of Matthew
relates a parable of Jesus in which a farmer sows good seed in
his field, but while the farmer is sleeping an enemy comes and
sows weeds among the wheat. Richard Rohr makes this percep-
tive comment on this parable: "In a simplistic way we think of
the enemy as Satan. Yes, but it's also the world and the flesh.
It's the combination of all the lies of culture, the lies of history,
family, and our own brokenness, lies that we tell ourselves and
one another for the sake of some kind of minimal survival. We
ourselves sow weeds among the wheat, lies among the truth."[49]

The national history of selfish violence that Americans have
inherited and perpetuate is bewildering to survey. What should
be our attitude toward world domination, even if it is domination by the United States? Empire by whatever name, superpower or globalization, is inherently unspiritual and antithetical
to the Kingdom of God. Empire is based, without exception, on
acquisitiveness, coercion, ruthlessness, falsehood, oppression,
and arrogance. For Christians it can never ever serve as a justification for war. In its values and practices empire is the very
opposite of the Kingdom of Christ—the something "more" that
transcends time and space and shines with justice, truth, compassion, and joy. Perhaps Martin Luther King Jr's description of
God's Kingdom best identifies all that empires fail to achieve.
Empire never builds God's "Beloved Community" because it asserts the interests of a powerful few by wantonly destroying all
others and all else.[50]

In his book *The Heart of Christianity* Marcus Borg explains
the perception the early church had of empire by interpreting
both the Apocalypse of John and an early Christian acrostic.[51]
Borg understands the Book of Revelation as anti-imperial.
Among the things that John's Apocalypse reveals is the nature
of empire. In Revelation 17, John describes the Roman Empire
as the "beast from the abyss" that threatens death and destruction. The beast, empire, makes war on the Lamb and attempts

to annihilate what is good and holy. Borg correctly maintains that John's word picture "turns the empire's perception of itself upside down. In the myth of Apollo slaying Python, Rome saw itself as Apollo: Apollo was the god of light and order, and Python was the ancient serpent. But the author of Revelation reverses this: the empire is not Apollo, but Python. The empire is what threatens to plunge the world into chaos."[52] Not only does John portray the empire as the ancient serpent, the incarnation of Satan, it is also the "great whore." She is enthralling and seductive. She is exquisitely dressed. Her clothes and her jewelry are extraordinarily expensive. Indeed, we are meant to understand that the secret of her seductive beauty is in her wealth and power. She rides upon the beast and is the beast. She and the serpent are one. In John's vision she is also "Babylon the great, mother of whores and of earth's abominations . . . drunk with the blood of the saints." She is "the great city that rules over the kings of the earth." She is Rome. She is empire.[53]

Borg finds this perception of empire further substantiated in an early Christian acrostic. In Latin this early acrostic reads, *Radix omnium malorum avaritia*: "Avarice (or greed) is the root of all evil." The first letters of each word combine to form the word *Roma,* the Latin spelling for Rome. "It makes a striking point: Roma—empire—is the embodiment of avarice, the incarnation of greed. That's what empire is about. The embodiment of greed in domination systems is the root of all evil."[54]

But the Kingdom of Heaven, which Jesus said "is not of this world order," is the incarnation of that mysterious God who is Love, and who can only be known through love (John 18:36). The spiritual journey leads to a fork in the path where we must choose between Caesar and Christ; where we must choose to become either "citizens of heaven" or citizens of empire.[55]

· 4 ·

Demythologizing the War in Iraq

———⟶●⟵———

Woe to those who call evil good,
  and good evil;
Who substitute darkness for light
  and light for darkness;
Who substitute bitter for sweet,
  and sweet for bitter!
Woe to those who are wise in their own eyes,
  And clever in their own sight!
Woe to those who are heroes in drinking wine,
  And valiant men in mixing strong drink;
Who justify the wicked for a bribe,
And take away the rights of the ones who are in
  the right!

ISAIAH 5:20–23, NASB

Buying the Myth

The myth believed with unwavering conviction by those addicted to alcohol is that, if they only manage well, they will never experience the utterly devastating consequences of their addiction. Those who embrace the myth of the holy war, in similar fashion, believe that violence can be redemptive if war is properly controlled.

Thus, Diane Knippers, writing in the September 2002 issue of *Episcopal Life,* sees the just war tradition as offering moral guidelines for the use of force in a way that reflects the "cardinal virtues of justice, prudence, courage, and temperance."[1] Just war, as Knippers accurately explains, "requires a correct use of force by a legitimate authority to bring justice and peace. War must be a last resort, and for a just cause. In its methods it must discriminate between combatants and innocent civilians. It must have a reasonable chance of success, and it must be proportional in response."[2]

Obviously, the just war notion is far superior to the ideology of unfettered brutality. Nevertheless, in contemplating just war theory one is compelled to ask, "When and where has such a war ever been fought?" William Tecumseh Sherman, one of America's more infamous war criminals, said to the women, children, and elderly of Atlanta who were pleading for mercy, "War is hell! War is cruelty and there is nothing you can do to refine it."[3]

The belief that war can be just, redemptive, or refined is a myth. At this moment we are, as a nation, living that myth. Without demythologizing it, we risk blindly descending further and further into our delusional thinking and self-fabricated reality. The Iraq War was sold to the American people—who were eager buyers—as a just war. But how well does the real military campaign in Iraq meet the most basic requirements for a just war?

Requirements and Realities: A Legitimate Authority

A just war may be launched, according to Saint Augustine and those who have followed him, only by a competent authority, meaning legitimate leadership. According to the purposeful wording of the U.S. Constitution, the authority to declare war rests solely with the United States Congress—not with the president or with the Supreme Court, but with Congress.

Five times in the history of this country Congress has issued a declaration of war: against England in 1812; Mexico in 1846; Spain in 1898; Germany and its allies in World War I; and Germany, Japan, and their allies in World War II. On two occasions Congress refused a president's request to go to war: President Madison's request against Algiers in 1815 and Clinton's request against Yugoslvia in 1999.[4] In 1950, when North Korea invaded South Korea, President Truman arrogantly refused to appeal to Congress before committing American troops to that bloody conflict. Truman was fearful that he would not get a declaration from Congress—or would at least find getting one so difficult that it would mean serious political trouble for him personally—and that a protracted fight with Congress over a declaration of war might make it much harder to deal with such emergencies in the future. Bypassing Congress, Truman went to the United Nations and persuaded it to authorize an armed "peace-keeping mission." In an attempt to justify his blatant disregard for America's most fundamental document of liberty, Truman referred to the carnage in Korea as a "police action" rather than as a war.[5]

Although without any constitutional support whatsoever, Truman's political strategy became the precedent for the anguish of the Vietnam War. In 1973, antiwar sentiment was growing exponentially. Concerned that it had lost all control over the conflict, Congress challenged the president's authority to wage war by passing the War Powers Resolution. This resolution states that the president can indeed start a war without the approval of Congress, but if he or she does so Congress must declare war or otherwise authorize the use of the military within sixty days from the start of hostilities. If Congress does not give this authorization the president must terminate military action.[6]

In the thirty years since Congress adopted the War Powers Resolution, substituting it for the provisions of the Constitution, it has been largely ignored by presidents. This, however, does not alter the hard fact that in the American system of democracy the only legitimate, or competent, authority for declaring war is Congress—engaged in sober consideration and debate of the costs, risks, wisdom, and justice of going to war—not the president.

For weeks President Bush argued that he needed neither the approval of Congress nor of the United Nations to invade Iraq. We may find this an astonishing point of view for one sworn to uphold the Constitution of the United States of America. But perhaps it is not surprising coming from what, in light of the conception of presidential sovereignty crafted by the Bush administration, Noam Chomsky calls the "imperial presidency."[7] Bush argued that he had the authority he needed in the congressional authorization of Operation Desert Storm, which was initiated over a decade earlier. Later, Bush said that he would "consult" with Congress but that doing so would not affect his decision. In thus voiding his gesture to legal requirements of any relevance the very notion of a consultation seems diminished to an empty, cynically political charade.

In the end Bush did consult with Congress, and, with a blood-thirsty American public sending the president's approval ratings soaring through the stratosphere, Congress, to use the appropriate slang expression, wimped out. Our legislators gave him what he wanted, though, in his estimation, what he did not need. Congress's complicity in Bush's maneuvering was extremely disheartening. The ranking Democrat in the Senate, Tom Daschle, weakly whined that Congress would like to be included and consulted but that it would work with the administration.[8] As witnessed in his speeches and televised debates, early in his campaign for the Democratic nomination Senator John Kerry sought to overcome the momentum of Howard Dean by appearing to be against the war he had previously voted for. Once nominated, however, Kerry sought to broaden his appeal to undecided voters by presenting himself—in campaign speeches around the country, before the nightly television cameras, and in debates with George W. Bush—as one who, like the president, would have gone to war, it was just that he would have done a better job of conducting the conflict.

The writers of the Constitution recognized that war is a nightmare and that, beyond all its horror, war tends to concentrate power quickly and narrowly, so much so that it is dangerous to entrust its authorization to one person. The temptation to use human slaughter for personal gain by a powerful few is too great. Peace, freedom, justice, and the well-being of all are more likely to be secured when such decisions are made collectively by legitimate representatives of the people.

The sum of our situation is grim: The war against Iraq lacks legitimate, or competent, authority. It was not first thoroughly considered and then declared by Congress. True, in the face of the president's political bullying, Congress acquiesced, but it did not declare war. By acquiescing to Bush's plan, Congress sacrificed its sacred duty to protect the citizens of our country, not to mention those human beings around the world affected by U.S. military action. The precedent for a president to act militarily without congressional support has been strengthened. Great power has shifted from the many to the one. The potential for many to suffer at the will of a few has increased. Indeed, it is manifest now.

While accepted stateside, the illegitimacy of Bush's tactics was apparent to many in the international community. Bush's claim that the United States is obligated to enforce U.N. resolutions is not a credible argument. Only the United Nations itself has the authority to enforce its own resolutions. In fact, the invasion of Iraq took place over the objections of the people of this world as represented in the United Nations. "The only country in the world where a majority of the population supported the war was Israel and this is the one country that is not officially part of the coalition of the willing (for fear it will drive some of the willing into becoming unwilling)."[9] Although the governments of Britain, Spain, and Italy all supported Bush, the overwhelming majorities of their populations were opposed to the war.[10] No doubt this is what led Colin Powell to make that comic remark, "We need to knock down this ridiculous idea that no one is on our side. Many nations share our view. And they do it in the face of public opposition."[11]

Kofi Annan, Secretary General of the United Nations, told the BBC that the Iraq War was clearly illegal.[12] He was not venting his personal emotions but upholding the integrity of the U.N. Charter. Article 2, Clause 4 of this charter declares: "All members shall refrain in their international relations from the threat or use of force against the territorial integrity or political independence of any state." Article 39 established the Security Council as the legitimate authority to "determine the existence of any threat to the peace, breach of the peace, or act of aggression." In "The Crime of War: From Nuremberg to Fallujah," an analysis of current international law and wars of aggression, Nicolas J. S. Davies states: "Clearly the force of current international law on aggression leaves little doubt that our government is guilty of a serious international crime."[13] The war against Iraq is without legitimate authority. Therefore, it does not meet this first, essential requirement of a just war.

Requirements and Realities: Valuing Life

Competent authority first requires legal legitimacy. For those who believe we live in an inherently moral universe, it is equally necessary that the authority initiating and conducting the war be competent in the sense of being qualified, or fit, to lead.

Dr. Charles Swenson, professor of psychopathology as well as projective testing at the University of Santa Clara in the 1970s, used to say to his students that everything, absolutely everything, is diagnostic—the way someone walks, the way they enter a room, where they sit. It all provides diagnostic information that enables one to recognize characteristic symptoms or signs of health or disease. It is not helpful to constantly analyze and diagnose people. If we do so it is all too easy to relate to them as abstract clinical subjects rather than as real flesh-and-blood human beings. Nevertheless, the things people say and do can assume a clear significance in regard to their competence. In fact, the ability to read people—like doctors, lawyers, dentists, and school teachers—is important to the way we interrelate in our everyday lives. Behavior sometimes indicates competency in a way that is difficult to ignore. Jesus himself taught, "You will know them by their fruits" (Matthew 7:16).

During the 2000 presidential campaign, when Governor Bush was debating Vice President Al Gore, the issue of capital punishment was raised. Importantly, there was a moment when, in defending the frequency of executions in Texas, Governor Bush became rather animated. And then he smiled with what appeared to be satisfaction in inflicting the death penalty.

It is not Bush's philosophical belief in the efficacy of the death penalty that raises concern here. No matter how much one might disagree with the death penalty, it is still a position that can be rationally defended. The popular evangelical writer and thinker Francis Schaeffer argued that, given the value of human life, the death penalty is the only appropriate response to the crime of murder.[14] Although I disagree with Schaeffer I recognize his stance as one taken only after having grappled honestly with the deep questions of life, death, and punishment.

I wonder, however, what even Shaeffer would have said in the case of Karla Faye Tucker. Tucker was a drug addict and prostitute. Along with her boyfriend she brutally murdered her ex-lover and his girlfriend in Texas and was convicted for the crime. But her conversion to Christianity, virtually spotless disciplinary record, apparent rehabilitation, and dramatic personality transformation convinced many people that her life should be spared. Yet George Bush, as Governor of Texas, refused to commute her sentence to life in prison. Quite to the contrary. In a 1999 interview with correspondent Tucker Carlson, Bush mocked her. In that discussion Bush said, in an angry tone, that while he had not met with any of the people pleading clemency for Karla Tucker, he had watched Larry King's television interview with her. He said that he thought Larry King had asked her "real difficult questions like, 'What would you say to Governor Bush?'" When asked what she answered, Bush "pursed his lips in mock desperation" and whimpered, "Please don't kill me."

But the Larry King–Karla Faye Tucker exchange Bush described never took place. In the interview shown on television, Tucker never pleaded for her life as Bush described; for some reason, Bush fabricated her words and her expression. Bush's callousness in the face of her fate is cruelly arrogant. Tucker showed greater dignity, grace, and honor than did George Bush, her "Christian brother," who held her life in his hands.[15]

I wonder if Schaeffer would have made room for the work of mercy and redemption in Tucker's case. Would he have acknowledged the divine grace at work in her life? Would he have argued for commuting her death sentence? We cannot know what conclusions Schaeffer might have reached regarding the case of Karla Faye Tucker. What we can safely assume is that Schaeffer, with his enormous appreciation for the immensity of human life, would not have smiled at her execution. Bush's smile is frightening. It indicates that something is not right when it comes to his regard for the sacredness of life.

Alberto Gonzales, now U.S. Attorney General, was Texas Chief Legal Counsel for Bush, and as such he was responsible for writing a memo on each death penalty case. On the basis of these memos Bush decided whether a defendant would live or die. Gonzales's memos have been examined by the *Atlantic Monthly,* which concluded, "Gonzales repeatedly failed to apprise the governor of critical issues in the cases at hand: ineffective counsel, conflict of interest, mitigating evidence, even actual evidence of innocence." In the case of Terry Washington, a death-row defendant with the communication skills of a seven-year-old, Gonzales only fleetingly mentioned Washington's limited mental capacity while devoting one third of his three-page report to the gory details of the murder.[16] As White House Counsel Gonzales was the very person who had asked the Justice Department for an opinion on the power of the president to authorize torture in the war on terrorism. The memo itself concluded that, contrary to the federal torture law, laws prohibiting the torture of enemy combatants during interrogation do not apply to the president. Gonzales argued that the Geneva Convention is obsolete and quaint.[17] His thinking is evil; but it is the kind of thinking in which Bush has chosen to immerse himself. The issue is serious. We are considering the moral qualifications—the spirit—of the man who leads our nation's military, and whose actions as president have led to the deaths of many thousands of people. The leader of a just war must recognize the value of human life.

There are other indications that President Bush has not developed an appreciation for life—what Albert Schweitzer called a "reverence for life." Yet to be qualified to lead a just war Bush must be able to see the value of every human being and to speak out of that recognition. What kind of person declares to voters that Jesus is his hero and then asks for his enemy's head on dry ice in a cardboard box?[18] What is missing from the heart of a person—what has happened to his fundamental humanity—when his first uncensored reaction to the image of that plane exploding into the World Trade Center is not one of horror at the human tragedy, but to quip: "That's one terrible pilot"?[19] Does the president inspire confidence in his values when he taunts Iraqi fighters, cheering to television crews, "Bring it on!"? Further, Bush's support of Defense Secretary Donald Rumsfeld after the torture of Iraqi prisoners became public knowledge, and Rumsfeld's own cavalier and jocular attitude in his public relations appearance at Abu Ghraib and before American troops in Iraq, is alarming.[20] Not only does it communicate a disturbing arrogance and untouchability about Bush and the kind of people gathered around him; such swagger sends an implicit message to American troops about the treatment of those they hold captive. Respect and dignity and humane treatment do not apply.

Bush's refusal to say that torture is never justified when pointedly asked at the G8 Conference was stunning.[21] We will never know all the ramifications of Bush's response (or choice not to respond, if that was the case) to the Justice Department memo arguing that as president he had the right to authorize torture. We will never know what his actions did to promote a climate hospitable to cruelty and murder. But is it possible to imagine Jesus of Nazareth not rejecting such an assertion as repugnant to the God who made and loves us all? Is it conceivable that Jesus would not have reprimanded any disciple who made such a proposal, especially in such strong and unambiguous language?[22]

But not our president. Bush chose not to distance himself from the ranting of Rush Limbaugh, radio commentator on the radical right, when Limbaugh characterized the torture of Iraqis by American soldiers as our troops just letting off some steam.[23] Conceding to public opinion, the president did say that the use of torture (which he euphemistically called "abuse") was disgusting. It did not represent, he said, however, the true character of Americans. But U.S. actions in Peleliu, No Gun Ri, My Lai, the rampage of the Tiger Force in the highlands of Vietnam, and Dashtai-Leili remind us that the use of torture is neither new nor unprecedented in our history, our memory, or our current military leadership. For example, the U.S. uses a small fleet of executive jets to fly terrorist suspects seized by the CIA to prisons in countries infamous for torture. Masked men grab people, perhaps entirely innocent, blindfold them, cut off their clothes and put them in a jumpsuit, tranquilize them, and put them on a jet to a place where there are no laws—a place where there is no human mercy for the guilty or the innocent. Michael Scheuer, until recently a senior CIA official in the counterterrorist center, was asked about obtaining information by torture: "And if some of that useful information is gleaned by torture, that's OK?" asked Scott Pelley of *60 Minutes*. "It's OK with me," said Scheuer. "I'm responsible for protecting the American people."[24] Does the sickening revulsion I feel at Scheuer's words indicate that he has committed what the Bible would call an abomination? It is a sacrilege to justify the practice of torture in the name of protecting any follower of Jesus. Unspeakable anti-Christian cruelty is not foreign to the character of the American people or its presidents.

The strange, flippant way Bush referred to the assassination of certain Al Qaeda leaders in his State of the Union Address was deeply disturbing. It indicates a terrible poverty of intellect and, more importantly, of spirit. Nee To-Sheng, the Christian pastor who was imprisoned because of his faith for thirty-five years and died in prison, wisely wrote:

> Is there life in me? Do I touch life in another? These are the questions. For life is something deeper than thought, more real than feeling or doctrine. Where there is life there is God. . . . But if this is the church's work and ministry, we can readily see what will be the nature of Satan's attack upon her. Death will be the weapon. . . . Life cannot be explained. When we touch it we know it is life. . . . Those who know, know. Those who don't, don't. Those who know can never explain to those who don't—until they themselves know. Those who know life recognize it in others. Those who have death in themselves recognize neither life nor death.[25]

In the same way, creating a deck of cards out of the list of Iraqi officials and military officers Bush wanted apprehended is not a sign of a healthy mind or a Christian spirit. Death is not a game. In fact, the jubilant, festive, playful atmosphere generated by President Bush, Vice President Dick Cheney, and Secretary

Donald Rumsfeld prior to and during the invasion of Iraq—and spread so readily by the media—is troubling to people of faith, compassion, and truth. When Baghdad collapsed in chaos Bush said that he did not see anarchy and rioting but people celebrating their liberation. When it came time for him to announce the success of the military, he strutted around in a flight suit on the deck of an aircraft carrier as if he himself—the very one who used family influence to stay safely at home rather than face the dangers of a real soldier in Vietnam—was some sort of a hero by ordering the final devastation of a starving people and an anemic military. What everyone is now well aware of is that the whole scene on the aircraft carrier was just that, a carefully choreographed stage production to sell George Bush as the savior of America.[26]

Requirements and Realities: A Wise Leader

In a thousand little points of darkness President Bush shows his disrespect for others and his lack of wisdom—the kind that comes from deep listening. Prior to the Iraq War he declined to meet with the presiding bishop of the Episcopal Church and leaders of other mainline denominations who did not believe that the violence toward which the United States was headed met the strong criteria of a just war. In doing so he deprived himself of the counsel of people trained in ethics, philosophy, and moral theology. Holy Scripture, which the president professes to honor, says: "Where there is no guidance, a nation falls, but in an abundance of counselors there is safety" (Proverbs 11:14). When asked if he would be willing to meet with people protesting the move toward war, Bush replied, "That would be like trying to make a decision by committee." He is simply unwilling to listen to anyone with whom he does not already agree. This is tragic because openness and receptivity are essential in the pursuit of wisdom. George W. Bush, then, is not competent in those spiritual values and skills of leadership that matter most.

Here is another pertinent issue in regard to competency in the sense of being qualified—intellectual fitness. Paul O'Neill, in *The Price of Loyalty*, describes one Cabinet meeting like this: "Everybody played their parts: literally. For this president, Cabinet meetings and the many midsize to large meetings he attended were carefully scripted."[27] Apparently it is common practice in the Bush administration to tell Cabinet secretaries before meetings what they are to talk about and when. O'Neill was disappointed to find the president, as would be typical in so many meetings, "virtually disengaged." The Cabinet secretaries who had come to this meeting, says O'Neill, had worked long hours to produce detailed reports, but the President had no questions to raise. Colleagues in the White House had actually told O'Neill that the president did not read reports, and it appeared to O'Neill that the president did not even read the brief memos he received. "This meeting," says O'Neill, "was like many of the meetings I would go to over the next two years. The only way I can describe it is that, well, the President is like a blind man in a roomful of deaf people. There is no discernable connection."[28]

It seems to me that at every level—constitutional, moral, spiritual, and intellectual, we must reject the premise that the war in Iraq is based on competent authority.

In the sixth century B.C.E. the great Chinese sage Lao Tsu was persuaded to write down his teachings just before he rode off into the desert to die, "sick at heart with the ways of man." His teaching—which, like that of Christ's, is the complete antithesis of Bush's philosophy—was contained in only five thousand characters that are divided into eighty-one chapters. In chapter 31 he wrote about war and victory like this:

> Weapons are instruments of fear; they are not a wise
>   man's tools.
> He uses them only when he has no choice.
> Peace and quiet are dear to his heart.

And victory is no cause for rejoicing.
If you rejoice in victory, then you delight in killing;
If you delight in killing, you cannot fulfill yourself.
When many people are being killed,
They should be mourned in heartfelt sorrow.
That is why victory must be observed like a funeral.[29]

In saying this Lao Tsu showed himself to be more Christian, more compassionate, more spiritual, and more competent than many professed Christians, including George W. Bush. By arriving on an aircraft carrier in a Navy S-3B Viking, which can carry nearly four thousand pounds of weaponry, wearing a flight suit and giving a speech in front of a large "mission accomplished" banner, Bush exalted the massive violence used to bring about this "victory."

Requirements and Realities: National Motivations

The values and the wisdom expressed by Lao Tsu are truer to the Christian faith, and to the spiritual ideals of all the great faith traditions of the world, than those expressed in Toby Keith's "Courtesy of the Red, White, & Blue":

And you'll be sorry that you messed with the U.S. of A.
'Cause we'll put a boot in your ass
It's the American way.[30]

To put a boot in someone's ass may be the American way, but it is not the Christian way. Nor is the Bloodhound Gang's "Fire Water Burn," which has been adopted by many American troops in Iraq as a kind of battle hymn:

The roof the roof the roof is on fire
We don't need no water let the motherfucker burn
Burn motherfucker burn.[31]

The spirit expressed in these lyrics and embraced by many Americans and many in its army can only be described as demonic. It expresses a lust for vengeance and destruction that is entirely alien to the humanitarian motives of peace and justice that are claimed to underlie just war theory.

A just war, according to many theologians and philosophers, must be based on right intention. This has come to mean that war is never justified if it is motivated by desire for gain, or glory, or revenge. In *Before the Dawn* Eugenio Zolli writes this pertinent paragraph explaining his conversion to Christianity immediately after World War II:

> I began to be conscious of a God whom I loved, One who wants to be loved and who Himself loves. I said to myself: From the beginning of the world men have killed themselves and made their fellow men suffer. They destroy their own lives in order to possess a river, a mountain, a pipeline, a market—and even for the sake of religious doctrines. And sometimes a race comes to regard itself as more gifted and more powerful than all others, and sees in this a sign of election, finding in it a new reason to kill. I began to feel more and more keenly the desire to find someone who would speak to me of the God of Love, the God who loves all without distinction and desires that the bonds which unite men should be those of love.[32]

A just war, then, is a war of last resort; that is, it is engaged in for the sole purpose of self-defense. Bush and his cohorts have given many reasons for invading Iraq. Those most openly and publicly announced were to eliminate the "imminent threat" of Saddam Hussein and his huge stockpile of weapons of mass destruction, to liberate the Iraqi people from their suffering under the Baathists, and to effectively combat terrorism. Similar, but also in addition to these reasons, are five others attributed to Dick Cheney, Donald Rumsfeld, Paul Wolfowitz (former Deputy

Secretary of Defense and current president of the World Bank), and George Bush by White House insiders:

- To clean up the mess left by the first Bush administration when, in 1991, it let Saddam Hussein consolidate power and slaughter opponents after the first U.S.–Iraq War.
- To improve Israel's strategic position by eliminating a large, hostile military force in the region.
- To create an Arab democracy that could serve as a model to other friendly Arab states now threatened with internal dissent, notably Egypt and Saudi Arabia.
- To permit the withdrawal of U.S. forces from Saudi Arabia (after twelve years), where they were stationed to counter the Iraqi military and were a source of anti-Americanism threatening the region.
- To create another friendly source of oil for the U.S. market and reduce dependency upon oil from Saudi Arabia, which might suffer overthrow someday.[33]

1. Clean Up the Mess

I assume that the mess Bush, Cheney, Rumsfeld, and Wolfowitz were talking about was not seizing Baghdad itself and occupying the whole of Iraq at the end of the Gulf War. George W. Bush appears to have been personally embarrassed by his father leaving a defiant Hussein in power. Ultimately, the question is not whether the first President Bush created a mess by launching the Gulf War, but that going to war to eradicate any sign of defiance or independence on the part of another country, or its leaders, hardly meets the requirements of a just war. Neither an insatiable desire to dominate and control nor the fury that may fuel it can ever form the right intention of just war.

Humanitarian concerns have frequently been linked to, or even offered as part of, this "cleaning up the mess" rationale.

It must certainly be acknowledged that war as a humanitarian intervention has been given a large place by moral philosophers and just war advocates. But in the same way that there are requirements that must be met in order for a war to be deemed just, so there are specific criteria for determining whether a particular military action is a humanitarian intervention. Ken Roth, in writing for Human Rights Watch, has done an excellent job of spelling this out.[34]

Human Rights Watch accepts the premise that military force may be necessary but only where there is an ongoing or imminent threat of genocide or mass slaughter. Other forms of tyranny may be truly awful, but given the death, destruction, and disorder of war, they do not rise to a level that justifies military force if there is no continuing or immediate possibility of a massive loss of human life. It is estimated that during the last twenty-five years the government of Iraq murdered or "disappeared" 250,000 Iraqis. Roth argues that during the 1988 genocide in which 100,000 Kurds were slaughtered, a humanitarian intervention would have been entirely justified. By the time of the invasion in March 2003, however, Hussein's killing spree had ebbed so that the necessary threshold of ongoing or imminent mass slaughter was not reached.[35] This in itself, says Roth, "was sufficient to disqualify the invasion of Iraq as a humanitarian intervention."[36]

Where this high threshold is met, there are five other factors to be considered when determining whether military force is justified as a humanitarian intervention. First, to qualify as a humanitarian intervention war must be the last reasonable option to stop genocide. Roth believes that if the purpose of the war against Iraq was really to stop mass atrocities, then at the very least indictment and prosecution, as in the case of Yugoslavian president Slobodan Milošević, should have been tried. Second, the humanitarian purpose of the war must be primary. In the case of the Iraq War no one argued that humanitarian concerns formed the basic intention for invading. If such concerns had been primary, then U.S. forces would have made it their business to secure the safety and health of the Iraqi people in the chaos following the fall of Hussein's dictatorship rather than securing the oil fields. Third, the use of the military must be carried out in strict compliance with international human rights laws and concern for the civilian population. Among the indications that the American military failed in this regard is this: As the U.S. army advanced through Iraq it used cluster bombs in populated areas, resulting in the substantial loss of civilian lives. One may add to this events such as the attack on Fallujah General Hospital because the U.S. did not like its reporting of the number of Iraqis that had been killed or wounded.[37] "Such disregard for human life," writes Roth, "is incompatible with a genuinely humanitarian intervention."[38] Fourth, the war must be reasonably calculated to make things better rather than worse for the people in the country being invaded. When one considers the present level of bloodshed and chaos in Iraq it is difficult to believe that anyone gave serious thought to the suffering the Iraqi people would endure as a result of the invasion and the continuous violence that has followed. Fifth, it is important to gain the approval of the United Nations as "a way to guard against pretextual or unjustified action."[39] The conclusion is simple and short. The war against Iraq did not, and does not, meet the tests of humanitarian intervention.

2. Improve Israel's Strategic Position

The invasion of Iraq as an effort to strengthen Israel's political and military position in the Middle East is the continuation of a decades-old U.S. policy and, therefore, it is new only in the sense that Bush and his advisers used it as a justification for war. While speaking to a panel of foreign policy experts at the University of Virginia on September 10, 2002, Philip Zelikow, a former member of the president's Foreign Intelligence Advisory Board, cast the attack on Iraq as one meant to offer greater security to Israel. "Why would Iraq attack America or use nuclear weapons against us?" he asked. "I'll tell you what I think the real threat [is] and actually has been since 1990—it's the threat against Israel."[40] Phyllis Bennis, of the Washington-based Institute of Policy Studies, responded that the protection of Israel was a component of the rationale for invading and occupying Iraq but not its driving motivation.[41] Others, like Nathan Brown, take the position that "all of them [Bush, Cheney, Rumsfeld, Wolfowitz, and Powell], were sort of fishing about for justification for a decision that had already been made."[42] Under the rubrics of a just war the defense of a weaker neighbor who is about to be overwhelmed by the superior force of an aggressor is justified. But it is difficult to imagine Israel needing any real protection. Israel has one of the best-trained, most disciplined, well-equipped, and ably led armies in the world. Its air force is superb. In the 1967 Six-Day War the Israeli military was able to humiliate easily and decisively a coalition from Egypt, Syria, and Jordan, even though those three countries were supplied with additional troops and tanks by Iraq, Iran, and Kuwait. Israel has been more than generously armed by America, and, although it refuses to acknowledge its nuclear capabilities, it is generally believed that Israel is equipped with the power to send the whole Middle East up in an atomic conflagration.

It may well be that the conquest of Iraq has improved the strategic position of Israel. But that is not the issue. A nation committed to the principles of just war does not use force to increase its own, or a friendly neighbor's, military dominance over the world or a region. Armed intervention is permissible only where a defenseless and innocent neighbor has actually been attacked or is under immediate threat of attack, which is certainly not what happened in this instance.

3. Create an Arab Democracy

The democratic ideal, the conviction that all people are equal and have the right to share in directing matters that affect them, is an intensely emotional issue and a deeply held cultural value of the American people. The fact that democracy as a value is so deeply embedded in our American psyche makes it a perfect instrument for manipulating our national will. Nearly twenty-five hundred years ago Alexander the Great energized the Macedonians and Greeks to conquer the world by envisioning Greek culture and ideals as religious and moral imperatives to be imposed on all nations and peoples. The feeling that one is morally or culturally superior is always highly seductive and easily slides into the belief that we are behaving nobly and righteously when we force others to adopt our cultural values. When Saint James says, "For where there is envy and selfish ambition, there will also be disorder and wickedness of every kind," he uses the same word for "envy" that is sometimes translated as "jealousy" and sometimes as "zeal" (James 3:16). The multiple significance of the word points to how our zeal for a good cause, or the right thing, can turn into an ugly and vicious way of thinking that creates spiritual chaos and disorder in all our relationships and loves. Once we tell people that they must either democratize or we will shoot them, we have abandoned the moral high ground essential to just war theory.

It is not so much democracy as a system of government but democracy as an inner orientation that matters most to those who think seriously about what it means to be a moral person. If democratic states are as quick to go to war as undemocratic states—and the statistical evidence says that they are—where is their superior virtue?[43] If the controlling political party in a democracy is successful in suppressing the vote of minorities who might cast their ballots for the opposition, where is the democracy?[44] If the leaders of a supposedly democratic government secretly meet with and are directed by a few executives of self-serving megacorporations to determine energy policies affecting every citizen—as was widely reported of Vice President Dick Cheney—then where is the democratic participation? Episcopalians vow in their Baptismal Covenant to "strive for justice and peace among all people, and to respect the dignity of every human being." Not only this, but they make the utterly astounding promise "to seek and serve Christ in all persons, and to love their neighbor as they love themselves."[45] These values are deeper than democracy as a philosophy or even democracy as a life principle. These are the kinds of values that give substance and reality to democracy. In an article called "Afghanistan Could Fail Again, UN Study Warns," Stephen Graham writes: "The report was also critical of the U.S.-led military engagement in Afghanistan, saying it helped produce a climate of 'fear, intimidation, terror and lawlessness' and neglected the longer-term threat to security posed by inequality and injustice."[46] The fact that Afghanistan and Iraq have held U.S.-mandated elections of a sort makes them neither democratic nor just. As nothing more than a political system democracy lacks the moral qualities to justify war. As a moral principle rooted in justice and respect democracy is a powerful moral argument against war.

4. Withdraw U.S. Forces from Saudi Arabia

The need to redeploy troops currently located in Saudi Arabia was another reason for going to war discussed among the troika of Bush, Cheney, and Rumsfeld. Although the Saudis and the Americans once had strong ties, relations have been strained since the September 11, 2001, attacks. Large numbers of Saudis have come to resent the continuing presence of U.S. military forces in their country, which is home to two of Islam's most holy sites, Mecca and Medina. Osama bin Laden even used the presence of American troops in Saudi Arabia as a part of his appeal for Muslims to rise up and join him in jihad. Furthermore, if Bush and the others are indeed considering bombing Syria or Iran, then having airbases in Iraq is far more practical and valuable than having one in Saudi Arabia.[47] The redeployment of American forces currently located in Saudi Arabia may make political, logistical, and strategic sense, but this has nothing to do with the self-defense or the humanitarian motives of a just war. I am, therefore, granting that attacking and occupying Iraq and killing thousands upon thousands of people may be militarily advantageous for an America bent on controlling the oil resources of the Middle East, but it does not rise to the ethical and moral standards of just war.

5. Shift Sources of Oil

While publicly denied or ignored by President Bush, invading Iraq in order to create another friendly source of oil for the U.S. was a major determinant in going to war, as White House insiders—and large numbers of private citizens using common sense—knew. And the corporate world certainly knew it as well. In Michael Moore's outstanding documentary *Fahrenheit 9/11* Dr. Sam Kubbar of the American Iraq Chamber of Commerce says: "War is always good for certain companies that are in the business of war. . . . If it wasn't for oil nobody would be in Iraq." In the same documentary, Youseff Sleiman, representing the Harris Corporation's Iraq Initiatives Office, crassly declares at a large corporate conference called "Rebuilding Iraq: We Are New-Fields": "Lots of money is there. . . . Once the oil starts flowing and the money starts coming . . . it's going to get better. . . . There's no question of how much money is there. . . . Whatever it costs the government is going to pay you. . . . It's going to get better, much better." And Gordon Bobbitt of the Kalmar RT Center, which specializes in container equipment for the military and sells its products to armies all over the world, categorically states, "There is nowhere in the world that the opportunity for new business exists like it does in Iraq."[48] William Clark sees the invasion of Iraq as an "oil currency war."

In conclusion, the Iraq war was designed to 1) secure U.S./ U.K. oil supplies before and after global Peak Oil (the point in time when the global extraction of oil can be expected to peak on a bell curve), and 2) to have a large military presence to 'dissuade' other oil-producers from moving towards the euro as an oil transaction currency. These are two crucial elements in maintaining U.S. hegemony over the world economy. Reconverting Iraq back to the petrodollar was not the critical issue, but preventing any further movement towards a petroeuro is a critical component of current U.S. Geostrategy.[49]

So when the U.S. talks about the necessity of protecting American interests, it does not mean the protection of freedom or of the lives of its citizens. Rather it means furthering the interests and guaranteeing the profits of big business through violence. It doesn't take a philosopher or theologian to grasp the gross immorality of the situation. It just takes a good and honest heart. How difficult is it to comprehend the teachings of the Decalogue? "Thou shalt not steal. . . . Thou shalt not covet" (Exodus 20:15, 17, KJV). Saint Paul himself says that covetousness, or greed, is idolatry (Colossians 3:5, KJV). Even under President Clinton the United States asserted that it was entitled to use military force to defend vital interests, such as "ensuring uninhibited access to key markets, energy supplies and strategic resources."[50] When a nation blows people up for its greed neither it nor its wars are just. It is, rather, a cruel and idolatrous nation.

In addition to these five reasons for invading Iraq Bush publicly declared his personal hatred for Hussein and accused him of trying to assassinate his father. No empirical evidence has ever been discovered that substantiates the charge, but even if there were, vengeance is not a justification for war.[51]

In the reasons given by the Bush administration, no mention is made of the attack suffered by the United States on September 11, 2001. In promoting the war publicly, the administration has asserted that the invasion of Iraq comprises the next step in an international "war on terrorism"; yet there is a sizable disconnect between Iraq and the terrorists. There is, for example, no evidence that Iraq has provided shelter and assistance to terrorists in carrying out their plans to harm Americans.

As for all those who died in the tragedy of 9/11, war cannot avenge or diminish the pain of their deaths. As Arundhati Roy writes:

> War is only a brutal desecration of their memory. To fuel yet another war—this time against Iraq—by cynically manipulating people's grief, by packaging it for TV specials sponsored by corporations selling detergent or running shoes is to cheapen and devalue grief, to drain it of meaning. What we are seeing now is a vulgar display of the business of grief, the commerce of grief, the pillaging of even the most private human feelings for political purpose. It is a terrible, violent thing for a state to do to its people.[52]

Roy's words further evoke the president's use of images of the American flag and coffins of the 9/11 victims in his reelection commercials. Yet oddly the Bush administration has discouraged media outlets from broadcasting images of the war dead as they return home.[53] As surely as a stricken nation needs a leader, Bush's use of the dead seems to have little to do with anyone other than himself.

The question for moral people is not only whether there are things for which they are willing to die but whether they are willing to maim and kill and savage entire nations to create a friendly source of oil for the U.S.; or to improve the military position of a country like Israel, which is notoriously guilty of crimes against humanity; or to better deploy American troops and mercenaries in a land that is not their land; or to topple a dictator while becoming complicit in the president's personal hatred and lust for vengeance; or to impose democracy.

Requirements and Realities: Plan of Attack

All indications are that the Bush administration intended to invade Iraq long before the Al Qaeda attack of 9/11.[54] Paul O'Neill describes a January 30, 2001, meeting the president had with all the principals of the National Security Council. The meeting began with the president asking then-National Security Advisor Condoleeza Rice: "So Condi, what are we going to talk about today?" Rice replied, in what was understood as a scripted exchange, "How Iraq is destabilizing the region, Mr. President." CIA Director George Tenet provided a grainy photograph of a building that he said the CIA believed might be a factory for producing either chemical or biological weapons. With everyone excitedly leaning over the photograph O'Neill interjected, "I've seen a lot of factories around the world that look a lot like this one. What makes us suspect that this one is producing chemical or biological agents for weapons?" Tenet answered by pointing out some circumstantial evidence that made him suspicious but concluded there was "no confirming intelligence" as to the material being produced.

> The President said little. He just nodded with the same flat, unquestioning demeanor that O'Neill was familiar with. But a new direction having been set from the top, this policy change now guided the proceedings. The opening premise, that Saddam's regime was destabilizing the region, and the vivid possibility that he owned weapons of mass destruction—a grainy picture, perhaps misleading, but visceral—pushed analysis toward logistics: the need for better intelligence, for ways to tighten the net around the regime, for use of the U.S. military to support Iraqi insurgents in a coup. . . . Ten days in, and it was all about Iraq.[55]

The complete absence of any sort of critical reasoning by the people present—Bush, Rice, Cheney, Tenet, Powell, Rumsfeld, and Joint Chiefs of Staff Chairman General Hugh Shelton—is incomprehensible and scary. The one exception, of course, was Paul O'Neill, who was later ousted by Bush. These people bear primary responsibility for our national security. No sane businessperson would make a major financial decision based on such tissue-thin information, but it is on the basis of this sort of superficial analysis and lack of solid critical thinking that we went to war in Iraq.

Shamefully, Powell went on to repeat this flimsy argument before the United Nations. President Bush and the hawkish people around him did not care what the facts were. They were determined to invade Iraq. What was going on was actually a lot worse than the shoddy interpretation of facts or mere intellectual ineptitude. On May 1, 2005, *The Times of London* printed the text of what is now known as the Downing Street Memo. This secret document is the transcribed minutes of the British prime minister's meeting on July 23, 2002. It reveals that President Bush was determined to go to war at a time when he was still insisting that he had not made up his mind, that he was still legitimately pursuing peaceful alternatives, and that he would go to war with Iraq only as a last resort. The strategy Bush had already adopted for justifying the war to the American people was to connect terrorism with weapons of mass destruction. Washington, the memo continues, was "fixing intelligence and facts around policy." It further indicates some concern about the illegality of invading Iraq. Nevertheless, the assumption of the memo is that the United Kingdom will take part in any U.S. military action. In short, the Downing Street Memo establishes that President Bush, Prime Minister Tony Blair, and the top people in their administrations are the kind of men and women who are willing to lie in order to justify the shedding of blood for gain.[56]

Shortly after 9/11, Rumsfeld asserted the doctrine of anticipatory, or preemptive, war in an interview with Bob Woodward.[57] The doctrine of preemptive war was actually drafted in 1992 by then-Deputy Defense Secretary Paul Wolfowitz for the first President Bush. This document, called "Defense Planning Guidance," has three stated objectives:

> Objective 1: Prevent the emergence of a rival superpower. "We must maintain the mechanisms for deterring potential competitors from ever aspiring to a larger regional or global role."
> Objective 2: Safeguard U.S. interests by exporting and marketing democratic values on a global scale, either by persuasion or by military force when necessary.
> Objective 3: Take unilateral action when necessary. In place of taking collective action through the United Nations the U.S. should expand future coalitions to be ad hoc coalitions formed to deal with a particular crisis. What is most important is that the United States should be postured to act independently in a crisis that calls for immediate and deliberate preemptive action.[58]

Ultimately, what this doctrine of preemption means is that the United States has cast itself as something beyond a superpower—an empire, that, because it has the military strength to do so, is at liberty to attack anyone anywhere in the world in order to enforce its will violently, making U.S. democracy a hypocritical, cynical instrument of oppression.

"American interests" is simply a nice phrase to use instead of "avarice." It is a rejection of the moral principle of universality in that it reserves the right to resort to war to the United States, or the president, alone. By "universality" I mean applying the same standards to ourselves that we apply to others. The Golden Rule taught by Jesus is not merely that we should refrain from doing anything that we do not want others to do to us, but that we should proactively behave toward others in the very same way we want them to treat us. "In everything do to others as you would have them do to you; for this is the law and the prophets" (Matthew 7:12). Noam Chomsky offers this insightful comment: "The principle of universality is the most elementary of moral truisms. It is the foundation of 'Just War theory' and in fact of every system of morality deserving of anything but contempt."[59]

There are people, however, who believe that a just war may be preemptive. Consequently, five guidelines have been developed to determine when preemptive violence is justified[60]:

1. The entity claiming that its attack is a preemptive act of self-defense should have a narrow definition of self. A war of preemption fought to protect or enlarge empire is not justifiable.

2. A preemptive war is justifiable only where there is fear of an imminent threat, meaning an attack that will occur within hours or weeks unless action is taken quickly to thwart it. This further requires clear intelligence showing that a potential aggressor has both the capability and the intention to do harm in the near future. The threat must be immediate and unavoidable. In the context of current world affairs the preparations by another nation to defend itself against an American onslaught does not constitute an imminent danger to the United States.

3. Intent and capacity to do immediate harm is the threshold for justifiable preemption. Intent is clear when an aggressor has done harm in the past or says it wants to do harm in the immediate future and has moved forces into position to carry out its intent.

4. Legitimate preemption must be likely to succeed in eliminating or reducing the threat.

5. A preemptive attack is justifiable only where military force is necessary to avert a devastating attack. If other means can be used to stop the attack, for example the arrest of the terrorists involved or the

interception of a weapon, then military strikes cannot
be used even though they might prove effective.

6. Preemptive strikes must be proportional and discriminating. They must not attack and kill the innocent, and the level of destruction must not exceed
   what was threatened. For example, the U.S. threat to
   use nuclear bombs if the Iraqis used chemical weapons on the battlefield would not be, if carried out,
   proportional or discriminating.

It is informative—diagnostic—that in arguing the case for preemptive military action against terrorists, Bush has never once
indicated that his thoughts or actions are guided by this sort of
moral philosophy. Nor does there seem to be any awareness of
the acute contradiction between just war, or just preemption,
and the above policy advocated by Wolfowitz, Rumsfeld, and
Cheney.

Indeed, the evidence is that Bush, Cheney, Rumsfeld, and
Wolfowitz were planning to attack Iraq before they had even
taken office.[61] Richard Clarke, National Coordinator for Security
and former counterterrorism czar for Clinton and Bush, describes how, immediately after 9/11, Wolfowitz and Rumsfeld
shifted the focus from Al Qaeda to Iraq.[62] The day after 9/11, the
president virtually ordered Clarke to find a link between Iraq
and the attack on the World Trade Center even though Clarke
was telling him that 9/11 was Al Qaeda's work, not Iraq's.[63]

The Bush administration was looking for an excuse to attack
Iraq, and it found one. The awful truth is that the war against
Iraq was not, as Bush claimed, a war of last resort or in defense
of the homeland. It was a premeditated attack on a nation incapable of any viable aggression against the United States, or
even of defending itself. In regard to enforcing the no-fly zone
since the end of Operation Desert Storm, General Shelton told
O'Neill, "For every missile they fire we respond by destroying
ten of their batteries."[64] Each investigation leads to the same

conclusion: The Iraqi military had been decimated by years of sanctions and bombings and posed no threat to America or to other countries in the region.[65]

A just war requires the use of military force to be proportional. To what was the U.S. response proportional? Iraq did not crash airplanes into the World Trade Center, the Pentagon, or into the field in Pennsylvania. Iraq was in no position to bring down the American Empire. Bush argued that Iraq represented an "imminent threat." But later he redefined the word *imminent* to justify his actions: "If we wait for a threat to fully materialize," he said before the 204th graduating class at West Point in 2002, "we will have waited too long. We must take the battle to the enemy, disrupt his plans, and confront the worst threats before they emerge."[66] As Rashid Khalidi points out in *Resurrecting Empire,* this was a revolutionary departure from the traditional American belief that the United States should go to war only to protect itself or its allies.

> As some of the proponents of waging war on Iraq have openly stated, the 2003 campaign was meant to be the first in a new category of war they advocated the United States should launch on its own in the twenty-first century. These were to be wars waged to assure that American values prevailed—as President Bush stated, "these values . . . are right and true for every person, in every society"—or as others perceived it, to guarantee the United States continued hegemony.[67]

But there is no evidence that Iraq had any plans to attack the United States or to do it serious harm. Iraq was nowhere the threat that Al Qaeda was and continues to be; nor was it a greater threat than North Korea with its developing nuclear capabilities.

The clearest indication of the depth of President Bush's understanding and of his own motivations came in Diane

Sawyer's interview with Bush on ABC Television. Sawyer asked Bush about the "hard fact that there were no weapons of mass destruction, as opposed to the possibility that [Saddam] might move to acquire those weapons." The President's considered response was, "What's the difference?" Then he added, "The possibility that he could acquire weapons. If he were to acquire weapons, he would be the danger. . . ." Valiantly Sawyer asked again, "What would it take to convince you that there were no weapons of mass destruction." Again Bush replied with his mantra, "America is a safer country." Finally in exasperation the President said, "I'm telling you I made the right decision for America because Saddam Hussein used weapons of mass destruction and invaded Kuwait." And so Bush invaded Iraq in 2003 because Saddam had used weapons of mass destruction in the 1980's and invaded Kuwait in 1990.[68]

No doubt President Bush's claims will seem to many people to be clairvoyant, or at least farsighted, and the doctrine of preemptive war to be a prudent policy. My point here is not to debate the "worldly wisdom" of such a course but to insist that it does not meet the standards of a just war. Nor does it represent the Christian way.

That there were no weapons of mass destruction is now beyond dispute, and the 9/11 Commission has established that there was, and has been, no collaboration between Al Qaeda and Iraq.[69] There was collaboration between Iraq and its ally the United States of America in the procurement and development of the chemical and biological weapons used against the Iranians and the Kurds, but no collaboration between Iraq and Al Qaeda.[70]

President Bush's advisors appear to have been conversant with just war theory, and so in his speeches the president referred to the invasion of Iraq as a war to bring peace and stability and to end suffering. He referred to it as a war of last resort and as being pursued in the face of a serious and imminent threat to America. But Bush's case was built on self-delusional thinking, deliberate lies, misinformation, and the manipulation of the worst fears of the American people.

Just war "requires the correct use of force. . . . In its methods it must discriminate between combatants and innocent civilians. . . . It must be proportional in its response. These principles reflect the cardinal virtues of justice, prudence, courage and temperance."[71] The just war ideal is beautiful. But war is ugly. It is bloody and brutal.

The just war exists only in geopolitical mythology. The idea that war can be virtuous or violence redemptive is an illusion of the sort that Saint James characterized as "devilish" (James 3:15, KJV).

Requirements and Realities: Success

One of the strangest principles of just war theory asserts that a war can be considered just only if there is a reasonable probability of success. The costs of the campaign must be carefully calculated. Deaths, injuries, and maimings inflicted on an enemy and suffered by one's own people in hopeless violence are not morally justified. This principle is actually far more complicated than what one might think, as Americans discovered in Vietnam and are rediscovering in Iraq, and it is frequently counterintuitive. "Mission accomplished!" a jubilant President Bush crowed, but far more American soldiers and mercenaries have now been killed in Iraq than died before the president's vain assertion that "the worst of the fighting is over."[72] Thousands have been wounded, many maimed for life. One new study shows that one in six veterans of the Iraq War suffer from psychological damage.[73] One must wonder what costs we failed to count before entering this conflict. Some reporters have begun to write about a growing indifference among Americans to our own casualties.[74]

It would seem that in one way or another war inevitably eats the heart out of people—even those not directly engaged in the fighting.[75]

There have been other unanticipated costs as well. A survey by the Pew Research Center has shown that as a result of American unilateralism—reneging on nuclear arms treaties, refusing to join the nations of the world in a joint effort to protect the environment, refusing to endorse and participate in a world court to bring war criminals to justice, going to war against Iraq, and demeaning our oldest and most trusted allies in doing so—we are now feared, mistrusted, and hated as a nation more than ever before.[76] Far from reducing the danger of terrorism, the invasion and occupation of Iraq have greatly inflamed the hatred and violent passions of the Islamic world. After at first declaring that the number of terrorist attacks in the world had decreased, the Bush administration has been forced to admit that the number of terrorist acts has actually increased.[77] If the purpose of the war was to reduce the threat of terrorism in the world, it is having exactly the opposite effect. We have, so far, created a very bloody failure.

> With our army stretched to the breaking point, our international credibility at an all-time low, Muslims further radicalized against us, our relations with key allies damaged, and our soldiers in a shooting gallery, it is as hard to believe that America is safer for the invasion as it is to believe that President Bush had good intelligence on weapons of mass destruction or that "this country was threatened with Saddam Hussein in power."[78]

In Iraq itself events are clearly beyond American control. American generals boast that they will pacify a city and bring defiant "insurgents" to justice, then withdraw in impotence. They boldly declare that the rebellious cleric Muqtada al-Sadr will either be arrested or killed, and then negotiate a truce that enhances his power and leaves his militia intact. This and the assassination of one top Iraqi leader after another belie all claims to an evolving democracy or political stability in Iraq.

Our military resources are now stretched so thin and our diplomatic assets are so wasted that we are incapable of dealing effectively with the very real danger of nuclear proliferation. Indeed, America may well so exhaust itself in senseless wars—as have other empires like the Byzantines and Persians[79]—that it no longer will have the energy or the wealth to protect itself, or to promote a sustainable peace in the world, or even to provide for the basic needs of its own people.

Evidence of Our Values

I remember watching television shortly after the invasion of Iraq began. A young, handsome, articulate combat pilot, Lieutenant Gary Crowder, was being interviewed. When he was asked about civilian casualties, he said, "Civilian casualties are regrettable and tragic, but when you go to war they are inevitable. At some point you just have to stand up for higher values." I assume that by "higher values" Lieutenant Crowder meant living by the Military Code of Conduct: bravery in battle, loyalty to one's fighting comrades, patriotism, and conducting oneself honorably as a soldier. These are, indeed, virtuous qualities. But they are not, in Christian teaching, the highest values to which we may aspire. Christians look instead to divine communion; *agape* love for friends *and* enemies; faith in the way of Christ; mystical hope in the providence of God; willingness rather than willfulness; and gentleness, humility, and peace instead of violence.

The American military and much of the media, with which it was "in bed," expressed their true values by speaking so fondly, so proudly, of the "shock and awe"—the hell—they were unleashing on Iraqis. I doubt, however, that any of them would have found "shock and awe" to be such a happy and poetic phrase if it had been their children, their husbands and wives, their mothers and fathers and grandparents who were being subjected to this incomprehensible terror.

These are not the higher values that come from living in conscious contact with God. Henry David Thoreau's commentary on human values in *Walden* does not go down easily, but it is good medicine:

> The universe is wider than our views of it. . . . Every person is the lord of a realm beside which the earthly empire of the Czar is but a petty state, a hummock left by the ice. Yet some can be patriotic who have no *self-respect,* and sacrifice the greater to the less. They love the soil which makes their graves, but have no sympathy with the spirit which may still animate their clay. Patriotism is a maggot in their heads.[80]

We are brought back to the primal question of the Hebrew and Christian Scriptures—who is Lord? To paraphrase the theologian Paul Tillich, when our ultimate concern is less than the Ultimate we are guilty of idolatry.[81]

We have no way of knowing how many Iraqi civilians or military personnel perished in this deadly campaign of unrelenting terror. We do not really know because the United States chose not to count the dead.[82] It is easier to think well of ourselves if we do not have to see the ghastly corpses piled high. So too is it easier to keep people in a positive state of mind about the war effort if they can be prevented from seeing their young men and women coming home in flag-draped coffins.[83]

We do know that after a decade of sanctions that prevented food and medicine from getting into the country, after a decade of bombing, after deliberately destroying sewage treatment plants around the country to contaminate drinking water with deadly bacteria,[84] hundreds of thousands of innocent Iraqis are dead. Struggling to maintain the justice of the invasion, Bush argued that he was acting as a friend of the Iraqi people. But an editorial in a fall 2003 issue of the *Christian Century* offers an alternative view:

> In making his case for a preemptive strike against Saddam, President Bush insisted that "America is a friend of the people of Iraq." But James Jennings, president of Conscience International, has another perspective: "Try telling that to a friend of mine in Baghdad who walked out of his house following a U.S. bomb attack to find his neighbor's head rolling down the street; or to a taxi driver I met whose four-year-old child shook uncontrollably for three days following Clinton's 1998 'Monicagate' bombing diversion. Try telling it to the mother of Omran ibn Jwair whom I met . . . after a U.S. missile killed her thirteen-year-old son while he was tending sheep in the field. . . . Try telling it to the hundreds of mothers I have seen crying over their dying babies, and to the hundreds of thousands of parents who have actually lost their infant children due to the cruel U.S. blockade, euphemistically called 'sanctions.'"[85]

At this juncture we also know that Iraqi prisoners of war have been tortured and beaten to death. We know that prisoners of war have been secretly held so that they can be subjected to more coercive methods of interrogation without their treatment being monitored by the International Red Cross. We know that even before the invasion of Iraq the media enjoyed speculating as to how far interrogations would go along a continuum toward torture. We know from investigative reports that Rumsfeld not only approved hiding prisoners from the Red Cross, but that he himself bears responsibility for their torture.[86] The fact that the U.S. Army has investigated the torture and deaths of Iraqi prisoners is of little comfort. It is very much like asking the fox if he noticed anything unpleasant happening to the chickens while he was in the hen house. It is rather difficult to see the virtues of justice, prudence, and temperance that Diane Knippers pointed to as characteristic of a just war in chapter 1.

The Price of Empire

What we are finally left with is the empty assertion that the Iraq War is just.

The hard truth is that there is no point at which it meets the standards of a just war. Indeed, there are a number of ethicists who would simply say that war is inherently immoral and, therefore, all talk of just war fails to deal with reality.[87]

And that is my point. By demythologizing the war in Iraq, I want to show there are no just wars.

Rashid Khalidi observes that the historic reality is that while European nations—Britain and France—were able to overwhelm the military resistance they encountered in the Middle East, they were unable to dominate the region without paying an exorbitant price. "This is a price," he writes, "in lives, in treasure, and in reputation that we as Americans should think very carefully about before submitting to the siren's call that empire is easy and cheap, and that in any case the price is worth paying."[88] Beyond this, we have to ask ourselves what we are willing to give in exchange for our souls.

Out of the September 11, 2001, tragedies a marvelous opportunity for engaging in a courageous and thoughtful moral inventory was created, but neither the Christian community nor the United States as a whole took that opportunity. To recognize "our own complicity in the ills of the world"[89] is always redemptive. It is the difficult practice of reflective repentance, not easy self-justification that leads to progress on every level. Unacknowledged avarice, arrogance, and aggression will lead to the inevitable decline and fall of the American Empire as it has with all the others before it. That our empire is pure and our wars holy is a seductive myth, which, when embraced and caressed, will destroy us.

· 5 ·

Confronting the Hypothetical Dilemma

———❦———

My dear friends, I am not writing anything new here. This is the oldest commandment in the book, and you have known it from day one. It's always been implicit in the Message you have heard. On the other hand, perhaps it is new, freshly minted as it is in both Christ and you—the darkness on its way out and the True Light already blazing!

Anyone who claims to live in God's light and hates a brother or sister who dwells in God's light is still in the dark, stumbling around in the dark, doesn't know which end is up, blinded by the darkness.

1 JOHN 2:2–11, MESSAGE

What Would You Do?

The previous chapter focused on the war in Iraq as a kind of case study in which the best arguments for military violence could be explored. But the overall focus of the book is pacifism as a matter of conscience—a matter of *Christian* conscience. It is about the outward practice and the inner reality of love as the center of Christian spirituality.

In 1983 the Mennonite scholar John Howard Yoder published a thoughtful little book called *What Would You Do? A Serious Answer to a Standard Question.*[1] In his book Yoder considers the most common and persistent challenge to the pacifist position. The hypothetical question posed as a dilemma for the pacifist is: "What would you do if a criminal pulled a gun and threatened to kill your wife (or daughter or sister or mother)?" The dilemma is meant to prove that the pacifist is really not a pacifist at all and is therefore illogical in rejecting war. Alternatively, the question can cast the committed pacifist in a morally reprehensible light for not killing to protect an innocent victim who is part of his or her own family. What follows here is a recapitulation of Yoder's considered response to this question, along with some of my own observations and reflections.

To begin with, Yoder maintains that in order to answer the question seriously we must examine the presuppositions upon which it is based. "No situation," he says, "interprets itself."[2] There is no abecedarian, no elemental situation that dictates a particular course of action. Consequently, before answering what we would do if a madman were attacking our family, we must first recognize and name the assumptions inherent in the question. Yoder identifies six presuppositions of the "What if . . . ?" question.

1. Determinism

The manner in which the question is posed presupposes a closed, mechanistic, deterministic world. It assumes that the attacker is incapable of making any other decision, acting in any other way, or following any path other than the one leading to the evil that he is mindlessly fixated on. Neither does the question allow for any response from the intended victim.

We have learned from family systems theory, however, that no event is the result of simple cause and effect, or even of a linear chain reaction. Instead, every event is the product of complex and interlocking systems. A touchdown pass is not as simple as the quarterback accurately throwing the football downfield to a receiver who catches it and runs in for the score. Every play, the time between every play, involves a staggering number of interactions on the field. In this hypothetical situation there are at least three people present. Each of them faces not just one or two choices, but multiple possibilities.

It is even more difficult to apply the simple mechanical model of our hypothetical question to war. All the parties and their staffs are attempting to guess what others might do, or how they might respond to various scenarios. I first realized this while watching the film *Midway*, the fictionalized account of the famous World War II naval battle in which the Japanese and American fleets fight it out from aircraft carriers spread over a wide distance. In this film one sees skilled strategizing, brilliant tactical decisions, and wonderful displays of personal courage and character; but ultimately the outcome depends on good guessing and on a fortuitous clearing of the clouds at just the right moment. I had much of the same feeling in watching *Master and Commander: Far Side of the Sea*. One may make guesses and even plan for various contingencies, but in the end the outcome remains unpredictable. No one knows for sure what will happen if one move rather than another is made. Everyone's decision affects everyone else's decision, and every decision, every action, is constantly changing the situation.

2. Control

As stated, the dilemma assumes that I, as the one being questioned, am in control of the situation and its outcome. I have the power to stop the attacker if I choose to do so. In real life the situation is not that simple. In some cases it may be possible for me to succeed in stopping an assailant, but in others I may fail.

It is, in fact, unlikely that I will be able to stop a well-prepared, armed, and determined attacker who suddenly breaks into my home.

Joseph Swaim tells the true story of a man who slept with a loaded revolver under his pillow in *War, Peace, and the Bible*. When asked, "Aren't you afraid that the mere possession of it might provoke violence on the part of an intruder?" He answered, "I feel that I must do it. I owe it to my family to protect them in that way." Four months after this conversation his wife called her pastor asking him to come right over. "Someone broke into our house," she explained. "My husband took his revolver and started down the stairs to protect us—and they killed him."[3]

In most real-life situations the assailant has the most control. The Night Stalker of California was able to sneak into homes and bedrooms where he shot sleeping husbands to death and raped their wives. It is hard to imagine how anyone might protect him- or herself from the demonic craftiness of a Charles Manson. There are too many variables to rely on violence as a successful protection against violence. Yoder therefore writes:

> In any war at least one side loses: in some wars no side wins. On the basis of a calculation of the probability of success, the chances are less than even that I can bring about what I consider a successful result by harming the other party. This is true on the small scale because the attacker is a powerful person or armed for a premeditated offense. It is true on the international level because many dimensions of war cannot be manipulated with certainty even by superior power.[4]

The belief that we are omnipotent or "substantially in control" is the antithesis of any genuinely spiritual life. Indeed, very often the more we attempt to make things happen, the more we seek to control people and events, the more out of control and unmanageable our own personal lives, or the life of the nation, become.

3. Knowledge

No one possesses perfect knowledge about anyone or anything. What I find in my own personal life is that no matter how much I worry or plan, events simply do not unfold as imagined. I want to think that if I knew everything life would be less anxious, but what I find over and over is that it is not knowledge but trust that calms my fears. What I long for is not the impossible knowledge that makes the future predictable, but the wisdom that makes all things luminous and guides me in taking the right action in the moment. None of us knows all there is to know about life, about ourselves, or about anyone else. Yet, the "What if. . . ?" question assumes virtually complete knowledge about how the situation will play out: I know for certain what will happen if I do not kill this person. I know beyond any doubt that he will do terrible harm or kill someone I love more than myself. I know for certain that by taking his life I can successfully prevent a tragedy from taking place. The reality is that even with the aid of powerful computers into which massive amounts of data have been entered, it is impossible to know for certain the actual outcome of any violent confrontation or any acute combat situation.

4. Individualism

Although unstated, it is assumed by the person posing this hypothetical dilemma that the decision to be made is entirely individual—that is, it presupposes that the only one whose will should be taken into account is mine. But "the person who is being attacked . . . is also a responsible being and should be part of my decision making process. . . . It would certainly be improper for me as a third party in the conflict to deal with her enemy in a way she would not desire."[5]

As a Chaplain Resident in a large metropolitan hospital I found that questions of suffering and hope were not theories but the constant realities with which I struggled. Late one night, after many hours of being with people confronted by sudden life-altering tragedies, I was walking down a stairwell where the only sound was the echo of my footsteps. As a way of comforting myself I was singing a line from "Amazing Grace": "Through many dangers, toils, and snares we have already come. 'Tis grace that brought us safe thus far, 'tis grace will lead us home." As I reached the second floor I had a moment of spiritual clarity. I saw that just as God had been with me in every difficulty and sorrow of my life, so for all the sad and hurting people in the hospital that night this was an opportunity to experience the presence and grace of God in their "dangers, toils, and snares." And I saw that what was required of me was to respect the beauty and dignity of their suffering, and the enormity of the spiritual opportunity that resided in all their agonized choices. I think that this is, at least in part, what Episcopalians mean by the baptismal vow to "respect the dignity of every human being." To respect the dignity of another is to respect his or her right to wrestle with, to make, and to act upon the deepest questions of human existence. To respect others is to see every crisis and danger they face as profoundly spiritual, and potentially transformative—not only for themselves but for the rest of humanity as well.

5. Righteousness

The dilemma supposes that I am a righteous person, capable of objectively sorting out, identifying, and balancing my own personal desires and interests against those of another. It doesn't take much self-honesty to admit how difficult this is for every individual. We all struggle on a daily basis with this very issue. Like most people I am full of rationalizations—full of good reasons for doing the wrong things. In college I was captain of the debate team. My debate partner was a redheaded guy by the name of John. John was smart, funny, and a genuinely nice person. We did well in competition, but I thought that we, that I, could do better. I thought that John was holding me back, so I complained to the debate coach that John wasn't willing to work on improving our brief or put real effort into researching the issue. But what I really wanted was for the debate coach to reorganize the teams so that Bill—a superb debater—would become my partner. I rationalized my shameful manipulation by telling myself that I deserved to be partnered with someone of Bill's caliber. I got what I wanted at the expense of hurting and alienating John and diminishing my own character.

Our minds are full of tricks, and it is extremely difficult for any of us as individuals to honestly evaluate our motives in even the smallest of matters. But "there is even less reason to assume that a center of political power is capable of standing in judgment on its own selfish temptation."[6] As Reinhold Niebuhr pointed out, "It is less possible for a group to be consistently unselfish than for an individual. The danger of being one-sided is increased where power is greatest and when capacity for self-criticism is least."[7]

6. Alternatives

As structured, the question leaves no room for any possibility of alternative ways of understanding the aggressor's behavior. One night I was the chaplain on call at an urban hospital where a man was brought in with a gunshot wound to his face. He had become heavily intoxicated and mistakenly entered the home of an elderly couple rather than the house of a friend down the block where he was temporarily staying. He was a large man. The elderly couple in their panic attacked him. He fought back. They believed, of course, that they were being attacked. As the situation grew more chaotic, frightening, and violent the husband grabbed a gun and shot the accidental intruder in the face.

But the "What if . . . ?" question leaves no room for other ways of gauging or interpreting the aggressor's behavior. As Yoder explains, "There is no possibility that the offender might be a Jean Valjean only looking for bread for his hungry children in the home of someone who has more bread than they need."[8]

Untying the Question

The "What if . . . ?" question at first seems to be an appeal to some strict process of formal logic, but it actually also relies on a powerful emotional argument that makes the use of logic and objectivity difficult. The question is usually structured so that it is tied to feelings of love and affection within the family and invokes the fearful specter of psychopathic killers and the trauma of sexual brutality.

It also invokes the question of who I am as a person. There is an unstated accusation here that if I do not respond to the threat with lethal force, I am not a "real" man. "These emotional overtones," writes Yoder, "are irrelevant to the discussion of the conditions under which it is morally justified in principle to take life, yet the question as put makes the most of them."[9] Also, the argument is frequently sexist. The potential victim is a dependent and helpless woman who needs the protection of a virile male.[10]

The argument is not as altruistic as it may at first sound. When applied to a war situation, it does not urge me to defend the wives and children that the soldiers of my own country may be attacking. In the personal scenario, it does not ask me to have any concern for the wife or child of the would-be assailant. What is being urged is in reality an "altruistic form of egoism."[11] Although it is covered with a veneer of "service to others it is still self-oriented in its structure."[12]

This is not to say that looking out for one's self-interest is all bad. But self-motivation above all else is not a solid basis for Christian ethics. In this hypothetical case, the potential victim is my neighbor, but the aggressor is also, in that moment, my neighbor. Determining how to respond ethically and morally is hugely complicated by my self-centeredness.

As Yoder examines these presuppositions it is clear that the analogy between self-defense and war breaks down in a number of places. He emphasizes this essential disconnect between self-defense and the waging of war. "Even if I could agree," he writes, "that it might be my Christian duty to defend my family against an attacker by killing, the fact that the analogy between the two does not hold means I could still with complete consistency reject all war."[13]

Self-defense and war differ in a number of significant ways. In the case of someone attacking my family, the lone assailant is the target of my violent act of self-defense. I am not, at least in the hypothetical case, running a risk of hurting innocent people. And I am certainly not going to go to this criminal assailant's home and kill his family or burn his house. But this is exactly what happens in warfare. The people who suffer the most are the civilians. Furthermore, the analogy has to be turned around. On the individual level I am defending against an intruder in my home. But in the wars Americans fight, we are the assailants breaking into homes intent on deadly business.

If I fight in my home to defend my family against an attacker, there are still laws governing the actions of everyone in the situation. For me to be found in the right, it will have to be demonstrated that the aggressor presented a genuine threat and was in violation of criminal law, and that my lethal response was in fact self-defense. In war, the distinction between aggressors and innocents is at best ambiguous, and there is rarely any court deciding whether an act of violence was defensive or wanton. In our hypothetical situation it is clearly assumed that the aggressor attacking my family is without cause or right. In war it is not nearly so easy to determine who is the real aggressor or who is in the right.

War and individual self-defense also differ in the matter of preparation. Most people do not turn their homes into arsenals.

Owning a weapon is deemed sufficient preparedness for an emergency. If I have a gun in my home and my neighbor knows about it, that may be enough of a deterrent to keep him or her from entering my home violently. On the other hand, he or she may make plans to enter, seize the gun, and use it against me. Likewise, the stockpiling of weapons by nations does not alleviate tensions; it enormously raises them. This fear becomes one more step in the movement toward military action with all of its bloody consequences. If I kill someone who is threatening my family, it is possible but not likely for our situation to escalate into still greater violence and bloodshed. But escalation becomes inevitable in war. For recent examples one need only think of Bosnia, Croatia, Kosovo, or Iraq.

Yoder argues that in the end there is no real analogy between war and personal self-defense. "Mohandas Gandhi and Thomas Merton, for example, were ready without embarrassment to acknowledge the legitimacy of the violent defense of one's family or self without seeing this as any compromise to their rejection of all organized violence in social or national causes."[14] Killing in defense of my own life, the life of a family member, or in defense of an innocent victim does not mirror what happens in war; therefore, it is not logically inconsistent with a pacifism that rejects all military violence.

Finding Alternatives

As already noted, one difficulty of the posed dilemma is that it assumes that there are only two possible alternatives in the situation. Yoder elaborates on this assumption by looking at a full range of possibilities.

1. Tragedy

The first possibility is that the attacker, like Charles Manson, will be successful in carrying out his gruesome plan. This is the horrible possibility that the critic of the pacifist's position is sure will come to pass if the attacker is not stopped with lethal force.

2. Martyrdom

The manner in which many Christians have met their death, the nonviolent way in which they have resisted "agents of evil," has made an immense contribution to the cause of God, to peace, and to the welfare of the world. "For ever after they are remembered with respect, and the contribution they have made to the good of humanity has been greater than if they had stayed alive by killing another."[15] I am thinking of people like Jonathan Myrick Daniels, an Episcopal seminarian, who in 1965 went to Selma, Alabama, to work for the right of all citizens to vote. On August 14 Jonathan and several others were jailed for joining a picket line. When they were unexpectedly released they sensed they were in danger. "Four of them walked to a small store. As sixteen-year-old Ruby Sales reached the top step of the entrance, a man with a gun appeared, cursing her. Jonathan pulled her to one side to shield her from the threats. As a result he was killed by a blast from the 12-gauge gun."[16] Jonathan is remembered and honored as a Saint in the Episcopal Church. In life and death he encourages us to find a better way.

A. The Victim as Martyr

If a defenseless innocent is killed, some will see it as the mindless nature of reality. Some will see in such a senseless tragedy either the cruelty of God or evidence that there is no God. But others will find in it renewed energy to work for the kind of world in which such things do not happen. Who can contemplate the human slaughter in places like Rwanda without descending into the deepest crevices of sorrow or without wanting to make the world a kinder place?

B. The Defender as Martyr

"But the more congruent application of meaningful sacrifice," writes Yoder (and here he is at his Christian best), "would be for me to intervene in such a way that, without my destroying the aggressor, he would refocus his attack upon me instead of upon the originally intended victim. To risk one's own life to save that of another is a kind of heroism which most people see as fitting when the danger comes from fire, a natural disaster, a runaway vehicle, or a military enemy." Consequently, it seems to Yoder that giving the intended victim a chance to escape by risking oneself is "the first logical alternative to the "What if . . . ?" question. "After all, death is not the greatest evil one can suffer."[17]

3. *Another Way Out*

We cannot predict the future with certainty. There are always more than just two choices; therefore, the possibility of some totally unanticipated joyful outcome can never be excluded. We can logically consider two ways that there might be a happy outcome in this situation.

A. The Natural Way

I might think of some way in which to disarm the attacker psychologically or emotionally. Yoder writes, "It might be a loving gesture, a display of moral authority, or my undefensive harmlessness which would disarm him psychologically. I might use nonlethal force or a ruse."[18] There are numerous accounts of people in deadly situations finding such solutions. I recall the story of a young woman who was attacked on her street one night. As the assailant was dragging her into the bushes she noticed that he wore a cross around his neck. Guessing that he might be Catholic she shouted at him, "Baby Jesus won't love you if you do this!" He let go of her and ran away. The Quaker Ruth Fry gathered dozens of stories in her 1939 book, *Victories Without Violence,* of people who found a way out of life-threatening situations without resorting to violence.

If we are seeking to follow the spiritual path of peace so that we do not automatically see violence as the answer, we are much more likely to be creative in our response. Yoder dramatizes this principle with the inspiring story of Gladys Aylward, a British missionary in Yangcheng, China, from 1930 to 1941. Her experience was fictionalized in the film *Inn of the Sixth Happiness.* One day the governor sent for Aylward to come immediately to the men's prison where a riot had broken out. When she arrived the governor told her that she had to go into the prison and stop the riot. He said that his soldiers were too frightened and too few to stop the fighting and killing that raged inside. Gladys at first fearfully protested. But the governor said that if her claim that her God lived inside her and gave her strength and protection were true she should be able to end the violence.

Aylward was pushed through the immense iron-barred door into a long, dark tunnel. She made her way to the far end and stopped just inside a courtyard full of raving criminals whose yelling and horrendous screaming created a cacophony of insanity. A dead man with blood still pouring from the wound in his head lay just a few feet from her. Other bodies were strewn around the courtyard. A man with a bloody ax was attempting to chase down other prisoners who, in their panic, were darting everywhere. The madman with the ax chased a group of convicts in Aylward's direction. They dodged around her and ducked away. The man with the bloody ax stopped a few feet before he reached Aylward and glared at her. Without having to think about it, she took two steps forward and ordered, "Give me that ax at once!"

The man gave her a long stare, and then meekly handed her the ax. She shouted at the convicts to form a line in front of her. She organized them to clean up the mess, and to arrange the dead bodies. Then she listened to their terrible grievances. When the governor finally entered with his soldiers she demanded that he make some serious changes. Provisions were made for the inmates to work and earn a little money with which they could buy food.

Gladys Aylward was a small woman with no weapons or soldiers for support. What she did have was an enormous spiritual presence. Among the convicts that day there was a Buddhist priest who had been imprisoned for stealing. As Aylward was leaving, this priest who was a thief said to her, "Thank you, Ai-weh-deh," which means "virtuous one." For the rest of her years in China Aylward was known as Ai-weh-deh.[19]

B. The Providential Way Out

The natural way out is not limited to those who think in Christian terms or who necessarily adhere to any sort of religious faith. But the providential way out is distinctively Christian. The natural way out "combines coincidence and imagination to produce a result which, although unforeseeable, can be explained after the fact."[20] But the classical Christian belief that the future is in the hands of God frees us from the assumption that there are only two possible outcomes.

To begin automatically with the assumption that there are no spiritually creative opportunities or divine possibilities is a denial of our faith, of God's potential to help us to know what to do. Yoder writes, "To justify a choice limited to one of two most undesirable outcomes which can be foreseen, and choosing the one which I feel would be least undesirable to me and mine, assumes that God has no redemptive intention in this situation."[21] Furthermore, the Christian's belief in the resurrection—not simply as an event that took place in antiquity, but as a present and continuing pattern of human experience—means that it is precisely in those situations where everything seems lost and hopeless that God's redemptive work ultimately shines the brightest.

4. Attempted Killing

Of the two primary outcomes our hypothetical dilemma takes seriously, attempted killing is the second. Attempted killing itself has two possible outcomes.

A. Successful

I may succeed in killing the assailant, believing that my action has both moral and legal authority. I will have acted in defense of the innocent according to "the emergency powers vested in every citizen."[22] A number of years ago my nephew, Bob, and his family went boating and skiing with another couple, Joyce and Charles, and their children. After getting their boat into the water Bob, his four-year-old son, Robert, and their friend Charles drove Bob's pickup back to their campsite while everyone else waited by the boat. As they drove into their campsite a man was rummaging through the trunk of Charles's car and taking things out. They parked the pickup and walked up behind the man. Charles demanded, "What do you think you're doing? That's my car!" The man whirled around with a gun in his hand. "I'm not going to jail!" he kept yelling. While Bob and Charles were trying to calm the man down, telling him to just take whatever he wanted and go, an older man with his two nephews saw what was going on and pulled into the campsite. He too tried to calm the man but the tension escalated with each second. The gunman was telling them that he was going to kill them all. One of the nephews of the stranger who was attempting to intervene was standing slightly in back of the wild man with the gun. He was able to reach inside his uncle's pickup undetected and to come out with a .357 magnum. "Mister, you can't talk to my uncle and brother that way!" he said. With that the robber cocked his pistol and spun around. As he did, this thirteen-year-old boy shot him in the head, killing him instantly.

It could be claimed that by killing the thief this boy prevented a tragedy of six murders, including that of a four-year-old boy. Even if one grants that with this killing a larger tragedy was averted, however, it seems to me that it was not averted altogether. This whole drama still ended in the heartbreak of death and lost innocence. Of course, there is no way of knowing for sure what the outcome would have been if this man had not been shot. We can speculate whether it would have ended in a greater tragedy or in some graced resolution, but all conclusions would be based on mere conjecture. The point is that the "What if . . . ?" question assumes, and it is an enormous assumption, that, as in this account, I will have no difficulty in succeeding in killing, and thus preventing the greater tragedy.

A. Unsuccessful

There is also the logical possibility that I may fail to kill the aggressor. If he or she has superior force and has come prepared for the attack; if my assailant "has the unthinking drive of the perverted spirit that can be diverted by neither pain or fear";[23] if he is, as the argument assumes, immune to reason; if he is a better shot than I am—then any effort to stop him may only make matters worse. The likelihood is that both the victim and I will be killed, and the evil is compounded. Recently, I came across the story of Ron Foster. Late one Mississippi night in 1989, after drinking with his friends, Ron Foster rode his bicycle to a local store with robbery on his mind. He was unarmed. In the store he jumped over the counter to rob the cash register but the clerk pulled a gun on him and he was able to take it away from the clerk and shoot him to death. Foster, who had gone out that night intent on robbery but not murder, was apprehended and sentenced to death for his crime. One can never count on the success of a violent intervention or calculate in advance the amount of sorrow in which it may result.

Thus the question of pacifism and violent defense actually

has not two, as suggested, but seven conceivable outcomes. They can be laid out as follows:

1. Tragedy

2. Martyrdom
   a. Victim
   b. Defender

3. Another way out
   a. Natural
   b. Providential

4. Attempted killing
   a. Successful
   b. Unsuccessful

Yoder ranks the possible outcomes according to desirability: Successful attempted killing of the aggressor (option 4A) is an evil because, by choosing it a life ends, precluding any chance of repentance and growth. The tragedy of the victim's death (option 1) is the most evil in the mind of the questioner who would urge a successful attempted killing of the aggressor (4A) as a means of preventing the tragedy of the innocent victim's death (1). Unsuccessful attempted killing of the aggressor (option 4B) is the worst since it multiplies the evil outcome in that both the victim and the defender may be killed. Martyrdom of the victim (2A), martyrdom of the defender (2B), a natural way out (3A), and a providential way out (3B) all represent positive results, or what Yoder refers to as "saving" or "happy" outcomes.

Reflecting on these options, we note that an attempted killing of the aggressor (4) closes the door to the saving outcomes of martyrdom (2) or of finding another way out (3). Yoder writes, "None of those can happen if I choose to kill. Does this also mean that I do not trust God to work things out (2A, 2B,

3B)? Does it also mean I do not trust myself to be courageous or creative enough to find another way (3A)?"[24]

For Yoder the renunciation of killing (4A) as a solution is "the path of trust and faith." It allows for the possibility of providence (3B) or martyrdom (2). It faces squarely and honestly the challenge of finding another, more creative, way to resolve the problem. It represents the highest form of responsibility because it prevents the worst from occurring—the unsuccessful killing of the aggressor who then kills both the defender and the originally intended victim (4B).

Christian Choices

Our discussion thus far has addressed our hypothetical question on the basis of logic. Yoder's intent has been to avoid any suggestion that Christianity is unrealistic in dealing with life. He also wants to demonstrate that there is nothing irrational about Jesus or his teachings in confronting violence. However, Christian faith does offer additional considerations when it comes to facing the hypothetical situation. It is to these more spiritual and mystical dimensions that we turn next.

1. Love of Enemies

> Christian love of the enemy goes beyond the bounds of decent humanism.[25]

Christian love is not a matter of establishing some sort of reciprocity or of attempting to be a good influence. Christian love, the love of our enemies, is a confession of God's reconciling work through suffering. Central to the teachings of Jesus is not only that we love our neighbor as ourself, but that we "love as Christ loved." Indeed, according to John 15:11, to love as Jesus loved is the "new commandment"—the new commandment that we as Christians seriously seek to obey. It is not only difficult to love the right thing; it is also difficult to love for the right reason—to love for the sake of Love. Gerard Manley Hopkins, cleric and poet, probed his own and our motivation for love in translating, writing down, and reflecting on this poem, which is often attributed to St. Francis Xavier:

O Deus, ego amo te

O God, I love thee—
Not out of hope of heaven for me
Nor fearing not to love and be
In the everlasting burning.
Thou, thou, my Jesus, after me
Didst reach thine arms out dying,
For my sake sufferedst nails and lance,
Mocked and marred countenance,
Sorrows passing number,
Sweat and care and cumber,
Yea and death, and this for me,
And thou couldst see me sinning:
Then I, why should I not love thee,
Jesu, so much in love with me?
Not for heaven's sake; not to be
Out of hell by loving thee;
Not for any gains I see;
But just the way that thou didst me
I do love and I will love thee:
What must I love thee, Lord, for then?—
For being my king and God. Amen.[26]

The inner journey is meant to take us to a place where we love for no other reason than that we have become loving. In the final analysis, Yoder contends, "The simple, loving Christian who has never thought through the situation but who responds out of God's love for him or her may well be nearer to obedience than those of us who think we must logically process the kinds of concerns about which I have just written."[27]

2. Following Christ before Social Unity

> The Christian's loyalty to the bonds of social unity
> is loosened by the decision to follow Christ.[28]

Jesus called his disciples to forsake not only wealth but even their families for his sake. This compels us to question the assumption of our hypothetical quandary that the first test of moral responsibility is to kill in defense of family. In his highly contemplative poem "East Coker," T. S. Eliot wrote of waiting in complete stillness without hope or love.

> I said to my soul, be still and wait without hope
> For hope would be hope for the wrong thing; wait
>   without love,
> For love would be love of the wrong thing . . .[29]

I find in Eliot's words a great and mysterious primordial wisdom that echoes Scripture and can only come from God. It is that strange, and yet divine, wisdom that says that it is only in letting go of everything, only in emptying myself of everything, that I can be filled by the Christ "who fills all in all" (Ephesians 1:23).Whatever conclusion we eventually come to in regard to the loyal defense of family, our moral quest does not begin with the desire to protect either ourselves or those we love.

3. Resurrection and Eternal Life

> The Christian understanding of the resurrection
> of the dead, of heaven and hell, and of eternal life
> also inform the approach to the "What if . . . ?"
> question.[30]

Although the Christian pacifist is not prepared to impose a Christian understanding of a transcendent life on his or her challengers in this debate, it can be asked that they recognize that "for those who do stand within historic Christianity, our beliefs may reinforce our readiness to accept the cost of obedience when confronted by a hostile aggressor."[31]

In Hebrew Scripture the word *obedience* means "to hear." It is an attentive and responsive listening to the voice of God. And in Christian Scripture obedience is to be understood in the context of belief, faith, and unconditional trust.[32] It is our willingness to follow Christ without knowing what will become of us or what will happen to us along the way. To many this will seem not only impractical but foolish. Nevertheless, I personally believe that to be a Christian is to be willing to become a fool in the eyes of this world in order to know Christ (1 Corinthians 4:10).

4. Sharing a Gracious Privilege

> Committed Christians see, in their life of faith, not merely an ethical stance in which they want to be consistent, nor a set of rules they want to be sure not to break, but a gracious privilege which they want to share.[33]

The question for the Christian is, "How can I be a reconciling presence in the world and in the life of my neighbor?"[34] It is not a matter of fearing and avoiding doing wrong, but of living in harmony with my conviction that a change of heart, even in an aggressor, is always possible.

Viktor Frankl, the Jewish psychiatrist who survived four years of horror in the Nazi death camps, maintains that "the individual personality remains essentially unpredictable." We not only exist, says Frankl, but we decide what our existence will be. "Every human being," he contends, "has the freedom to change at an instant."[35] Frankl cites the case of Dr. J.—the only man he had ever encountered that he dared to call a satanic figure. Dr. J. was in charge of the largest mental hospital, Steinhof, in Vienna, Austria. He did his fanatical best to make sure that not a single psychotic person escaped the gas chamber and became known as the mass murderer of Steinhof. When Frankl returned to Vienna after World War II he assumed that Dr. J., like many other Nazi war criminals, had escaped to South America. But one day while giving a neurological examination to a former Austrian diplomat who had been imprisoned in the infamous Ljubljana Prison in Moscow, he was asked if he had been acquainted with Dr. J. When Frankl replied that he had, this former prisoner went on to tell how he had known Dr. J. in Ljubljana, and how Dr. J. had been a wonderful comrade. Dr. J., he said, "gave consolation to everybody. He lived up to the highest conceivable moral standard. He was the best friend I ever met during my long years in prison."[36] As Christians who believe in radical grace, and are familiar with the conversion of Saint Paul, we live out of the conviction that a change of heart may occur for anyone at any instant. "For the Christian to bear the martyr's cross is to share in God's way with his world."[37]

If I hold firmly to pragmatism and the belief that the one thing that must not happen is that I suffer innocently, then how can I participate in or live a life that is a testimony to the redemptive power of God's sacrificial love? Recently my wife and I went to see the new film version of the musical *Phantom of the Opera*. The Phantom is ugly and murderous; and yet he sings of how this loathsome gargoyle burning in hell longs for love and beauty. "Love me," he pleads in a haunting melody, "that's all I ask of you." But can anyone love such a monster? Wouldn't it be utterly foolish to love this loathsome creature? When the Phantom sings his seductive song to Christine he wonders as to the secret that may lie "beyond the point of no return." In the end, when the Phantom has carried Christine off to his underworld and captured her fiancé, Raoul, in a noose, it becomes clear what the point of no return really is. Christine is given the choice of securing Raoul's release by becoming the Phantom's bride or gaining her freedom at the expense of Raoul's life. In the throes of her quandary Christine suddenly sings to the Phantom, "God, give me courage to show you are not alone." The Phantom, now liberated for love and beauty, begins to weep and releases both Christine and Raoul. The point of no return is the point at which we make an unequivocal commitment to love. It is that moment in which we consecrate ourselves to self-giving love. It is that instant in which we become one with Christ; and, therefore, full participants in the redemptive power of his sacrificial love.[38]

5. Self-Deification

> Christian faith warns me that I tend to use the self-centered control of my decisions as a tool of rebelliousness, as a way of solidifying my independence from my Maker.[39]

My impatience, my selfishness, my retaliatory spirit all warp my perception and feed my tendency to self-deification—the belief that I can create my own ultimate security by taking matters into my own hands. But this temptation normally occurs with great subtlety.

> The real temptation of good people like us is not the crude, the crass, and the carnal. The really refined temptation, with which Jesus himself was tried, is that of ego-centric altruism. It is being oneself the incarnation of a good and righteous cause for which others may rightly be made to suffer. It is stating one's self-justification in the form of a duty to others.[40]

Yoder's conclusion is compelling in its honesty and faithfulness to the best of Christian thought and practice:

I do not know what I would do if some insane or criminal person were to attack my wife or child, sister or mother. But I know that what I should do would be illuminated by what God my Father did when his "only begotten Son" was being threatened. Or by what Abraham, my father in the faith, was ready to sacrifice out of obedience; Abraham could ready himself to give up his son because he believed in the resurrection. It was "for the sake of joy that was set before him" that Christ could "endure the cross."

My readiness—not in the contemplation of my moral strength, but in confession of the nature of the God who has revealed himself in Jesus Christ—to accept that kind of love as my duty and privilege is founded in no craving for heroism, no self-confidence, no pious enthusiasm, no masochism. It is founded in the confession that he who gave his life at our hands was at one and the same time the revelation of that true humanity which is God's instrument in the world.[41]

In the end, what John Howard Yoder helps us see is that the only solution radical enough and creative enough to save us is Love, and that for those consecrated to Truth death is no defeat.

Epilogue

Because I am not a scholar this undertaking has not been an academic exploration of the causes and conduct of war. I am an ordinary priest with the concerns and passions common to priests; but, then, every Christian, as the Apostle Peter affirms, is a member of the "royal priesthood," with its priestly concerns and passions (1 Peter 2:5). Every Christian is a participant in a community of priests—a community of conscience. If the words of this book have been heard as a cry of conscience then they have been correctly understood.

Conscience is not about what is, but rather what ought to be. United States Attorney General Robert Kennedy was frequently quoted as saying, "Some people see things as they are and ask, 'Why?' I dream things that never were and ask, 'Why not?'"[1] That's conscience. What is revealed to conscience, then, is something to be actualized. Viktor Frankl observed that love and conscience are alike in that they both envision and anticipate something that is not yet real. The difference, he thought, was that love anticipates "a personal possibility," and conscience an ethical or moral necessity.[2] I am not so sure that the two can be that clearly separated. Saint Paul was emphatic in his insistence that every moral requirement can be summed up in the imperative to love our neighbor as our self (Romans 13:8–10).

Put in this way conscience may seem a terrible inconvenience and highly impractical. I am frequently asked, "What would happen if everyone was a pacifist?" Aspects of that question were taken up in chapter 5, and so here I will make only two brief observations. First, it is highly unlikely that the whole country will ever embrace a nonviolent religious faith, or follow the nonviolent teachings of their tradition, whether formally religious or philosophically humanistic, other than in the most nominal way. Indeed, it is difficult to believe that there will ever be a shortage of people who believe that the killing of innocents for the sake of empire is living up to a higher set of values. Second, the really pragmatic question is about the best way to live out the compassion of Christ as individuals, as churches, and as a society. "Our journey outward, as followers of Jesus, as advocates of the dream of God, as the church," writes Marcus Borg, "calls us to be a community of compassion and the leaven of compassion in the world."[3] The crucial question is, How can we do that? In discussing the dream of God, Borg acknowledges that working to enact the kingdom of God on earth may be a "utopian vision," an "ideal." Nevertheless, he contends that such work and thinking and feeling have about it what the theologian and social ethicist Reinhold Niebuhr called "the relevance of an impossible ideal."[4] Our goal as Christian believers is to approximate as closely as we can the redemptive vision of Christ for the whole world. That we cannot perfectly embody the ideal "does not mean that it should cease to be an ideal," that it should cease to be a divine guiding principle for us. To be a person of conscience, then, is to be committed to peace, justice, and love. "Lord, make us instruments of your peace," Saint Francis of Assisi prayed, "Where there is hatred, let us sow love; where there is injury, pardon; where there is discord, union; where there is doubt, faith; where there is despair, hope; where there is darkness, light; where there is sadness, joy."[5] In *Stages of Faith* James Fowler describes those people, like Saint Francis, who are at the higher stages of faith development as people possessing "a passion," a conscience, "for a transformed world, a world made over not in *their images,* but in accordance with an intentionality both divine and transcendent."[6]

The word *conscience* is from the Latin *conscientia,* which is a translation of the Greek *suneidesis.* "Con-" means "with" (as in "co-"), and "-science" means "knowledge." "Conscience" may, therefore, be defined as joint or co-knowledge. The basic idea in the Greek *suneidesis* is that of an awareness of something, such as an awareness of having behaved responsibly or irresponsibly in some decisive moment. It may also be thought of, as already suggested, as an awareness of something I am being called to do or be. Frankl said, "It is the task of conscience to disclose the *unum necesse,* 'the one thing that is required'"—the thing that I as an actual person in a specific time and concrete situation have been called to make real.[7]

Conscience has also been explained as self-knowledge. Certainly, our conscience involves an awareness of the incongruity between what we are and the highest to which we aspire, so that those inner discrepancies and conflicts are exposed to Christ's healing Spirit. Ultimately, however, self-consciousness gives way in the New Testament to God-consciousness. In the New Testament conscience is associated with the voice of God and involves the whole person in relation to the voice of God—to the mysterious light of the Spirit in us.[8] Conscience is more than an immanent psychological phenomenon; it always has a transcendent quality to it. When we hear the voice of conscience it is not merely our own voice that we are hearing. "What I feel that I ought to do, or ought to be," Frankl maintained, "could never be effective if it were nothing but an invention of mine—rather than a discovery."[9]

The discovery of what we are called to do, of how we are called to live, in our own time and place is made more through intuition than it is by logical analysis. Gerald May, psychiatrist and spiritual director, defines intuition as: "The state of apprehending or appreciation that occurs *before* any thinking takes place."[10] Intuition is an unconscious form of knowledge. It sees essential truths and universal principles independently of the senses or of linear thought processes.

Earl, a fifty-year-old carpenter and recent convert to Christianity living in southern California, was on a trip into Mexico. In Tijuana he saw children living in a garbage dump. His heart went out to them, and he said to his wife: "We can do something to help these children." They found a run-down "ranch" in Baja and bought it. He went down on weekends to fix up the main house. Soon his friends from church were coming along to help. People from other churches, including a congregation I served, found out about what he and his wife were doing and offered money, materials, and labor. That run-down ranch is now a large campus, a spacious home for numerous abandoned and abused children. Over the years these children have become carpenters, skilled laborers, dental hygienists, teachers, and doctors. Earl did not go through some complex thought process in order to arrive at his decision. As I heard him explain it, he was simply and suddenly aware that he was being invited to express his gratitude to a generous God for all he had been given by reaching out to these children who were uncared for and unwanted.

James, a recovering alcoholic I met while attending an intervention workshop, tells how he built a highly successful business, sold it for a lot of money, and retired early. After retirement he spent most of his time drinking at home. Since he did not experience many of the problems associated with alcoholism he didn't think he had a problem. He had no financial problems, he loved his wife and didn't fight with her, their children had been successfully launched into the world, and he had no legal problems, such as citations for driving under the influence. The worst thing he did was to fall asleep—actually he was passed out—in the recliner by eight o'clock every night. One day he poured himself a drink and started to sit down in his favorite chair when a voice inside said, "James, you're losing your life! It's slipping away." He walked over to the telephone, called a hospital with a program for the treatment of chemical dependency, and made an appointment to check himself in as a patient. For James there was no inner discursive dialogue taking place at his epiphany. It was a moment of intuitive insight in which he saw what was and what could be.

A nun riding across India on a train realizes that she is being called to leave the secure, happy convent and school where she lives and teaches and to go to live and serve among the poorest of the poor on the streets of Calcutta. It is not an intellectual decision made after consulting a vocational counselor, taking aptitude tests, or listing the pros and cons of various career alternatives on a piece of paper. It is an experience of conscience—an intuitive kind of knowing.

"What is known in spiritual traditions as contemplation," May points out in *Will and Spirit*, "is very similar if not identical to the philosophical term *intuition*."[11] In the Christian tradition contemplation is prayer in which we sit silently in the presence of God, forming no words or thoughts or images but gently letting go of all these rather than clinging to them, stilling our minds and bodies and hearts so that our prayer is a prayer of simply being.

In ancient times the word *temp,*—the root word in *contemplation*—had to do with making a measurement. The word *temple*, as David Steindl-Rast tells us, comes from the same root. He writes,

> It is the word most directly related to contemplation, and it conjures up associations with the temple-like structures at Stonehenge. Originally, however, the Latin word for temple, *templum,* did not mean an architectural structure, but stayed closer to the sense of measure. It meant a measured area. That measured area was not even on the ground but in the sky. . . . It was the *templum* in the sense of a section of the sky which the Roman priests, the

augurs, contemplated. That means that they fixed their gaze on it with sustained attention.[12]

"Contemplation," therefore, measures what is high above and what is below *together.* The earthly temple in Jerusalem is built according to the heavenly vision (Exodus 25:8–9).[13] The vision from above determines the course of action below. There are those who say that contemplation is a long, loving look at God, and they are absolutely correct. It is that sustained gaze at God that leads to wisdom of heart, to a conscience of compassion— the mystical knowledge of God's dream that we are to help make real in our own personal and public situation.

So the unifying theme of this book is the Christian conscience—a conscience that compels all who have heard the transcendent voice of God to do their best to love as God loves, to champion the cause of the poor and vulnerable, to pursue peace, to overcome evil with good, to insist on integrity and truth, and to vigorously oppose injustice and violence. Anne Lamott's summary interpretation of the teaching of Jesus succinctly describes this idea: "The point is to not hate and kill each other today, and if you can, to help the forgotten and powerless."[14]

Excursus: A Different Road Map to Peace

Among the simple but profound principles of both Hebrew and Christian Scripture is the teaching that those who have suffered much have a special responsibility to apprehend, to share, and to live out the wisdom of their suffering. This, in one way, makes the brutality and cruelty of the nation of Israel against the Palestinian people horrendously incomprehensible. How can a people that has endured so much agony inflict so much terror and injustice on another? It is absolutely dumbfounding.

Much of the American news media and many politicians contend, of course, that exactly the opposite is true. They appear to be engaged in a kind of tacit cabal, or complicity, of denial. Israel is portrayed as the innocent victim who unfairly suffers one atrocity after another at the hands of Palestinian "terrorists." Jesse Jackson got himself into public relations trouble while visiting Israel, because he wanted to recognize that the Holocaust was a great tragedy without saying that it was "uniquely tragic." Rudolph Giuliani, on the other hand, enhanced his image by going to Israel soon after 9/11 and asserting that Israel, like New York and the rest of the United States, is engaged in a just war against terrorism.[1]

Israel's influence on United States congressional leaders is unsurpassed. Its political action committees contribute millions to the campaigns of U.S. senators and representatives. Indeed, AIPAC, the American Israel Public Affairs Committee, is considered the most important foreign policy lobby in Washington today. Members from both houses of Congress, and from both parties, are flown to Israel by the dozens, where they can be even more effectively lobbied. "Don't worry," Ariel Sharon told Shimon Peres when he was anxious about the possibility of some bad publicity, "we control the Americans."[2]

Even a casual investigation, however, demonstrates that too many of the people of Israel have learned nothing from their suffering every imaginable atrocity. They have themselves become a terrorist nation guilty of crimes against humanity. For three days in September 1982 thousands of men, women, children, and elderly were savagely massacred in the Palestinian refugee camps of Sabra and Shatilla in Lebanon. The massacre itself was carried out by the Lebanese Phalangists, one of the many militarized political groups in Lebanon, who entered the camps with the formal approval of Israeli Defense Minister Ariel Sharon and did their bloody work with the acquiescence of the Israeli Army. As a result of his actions Sharon was eventually forced to resign as Defense Minister. He went on, however, to hold other cabinet posts before becoming Prime Minister of Israel in 2001.[3] Once again criminal cruelty was rewarded with power. The United States, which gave a written guarantee to the Palestinians in Sabra and Shatilla that they would be safe in the camps, repeatedly insisted that Yasser Arafat needed to go, but not Sharon.[4]

The media in America consistently downplays Palestinian deaths and the systematic targeting of Palestinian civilians by Israeli troops. To acknowledge these would be to admit that Israel is guilty of crimes against humanity. The story of an Israeli baby killed in the conflict is told in the American press in a way meant to elicit a sympathetic emotional response. A story about a Palestinian infant's death, along with the wounding of ten other children, is reported in a rather passive voice. She is not the

victim of ruthless "gunmen," as is the Israeli child. Rather she is
the collateral damage that must be expected as the Israeli troops
go about their security business. The U.S. media, relying on state-
ments from the Israeli government, presents the Israeli infant's
death as "a deliberate, cold-blooded escalation of violence." The
Palestinian baby's death is simply the result of justifiable retali-
ation.[5] One Israeli civilian is killed in Israel every seventy-one
hours and twelve minutes. One Palestinian civilian is killed
every eleven hours and fifty-seven minutes. In short, Israelis kill
six Palestinian civilians for every Israeli civilian killed.[6]

I am and have been a pacifist since I was baptized in my late
teens. I registered for the draft as a conscientious objector. I find
all violence abhorrent. I do not believe there is any excuse for
the bombing and killing of Israelis. At the same time it seems
ludicrous to argue that the Israelis are simply trying to defend
themselves against evil, freedom-hating Palestinian terrorists
whereas the Israelis are attacking and killing more civilians (a
frequently used definition of terrorism) than the Palestinians.

Since the beginning of the *intifada* in 2000, Israel has destroyed one Palestinian home every ninety minutes. On January 21, 2003, Israeli soldiers bulldozed sixty-two shops and
market stalls in the West Bank village of Nazlat Issa, depriving
between two and three thousand residents of their major source
of income.[7] Rachel Corrie, a twenty-three-year-old American
peace activist, was ruthlessly murdered by Israeli soldiers who
ran her over with a bulldozer as she protested the demolition of
two Palestinian homes.[8]

Israel claims that these demolitions, like the settlements—the
large housing projects built illegally on land confiscated from
the Palestinians—are purely for defense purposes. But Amram
Mitzna, the war hero and former general who ran for prime
minister against Sharon in the 2003 election, has categorically
stated that none of this really has anything to do with Israel's
security.[9] Nevertheless, Israel has escalated its apartheid-style
policies by beginning the construction of high concrete walls,

trenches, fences and guard towers that will eventually extend the entire length of the West Bank.

This wall, which is being placed on highly desirable agricultural land, will expropriate fourteen artesian wells in the Qalqilya region alone. When the wall is completed towns and villages will be isolated, farmers will need special permits to access their land (Israel already determines what crops may be planted), and travel documents will be needed to travel from one village to another. The West Bank will become nothing more than a network of prisons.[10] One would think the world had had enough of ghettos.

Actually, most of the world *has* had enough. The International Court of Justice has ruled that Israel must tear down its wall and make restitution to the Palestinians. The United Nations voted 150 to 6 with 10 abstentions in support of the World Court's ruling that the wall violates international law—that it must be dismantled and compensation paid. The United States once again voted for oppression and against human dignity by casting one of the six negative votes.[11]

Israel regularly violates human rights in the most egregious manner. Increasingly journalists are beaten and their lives threatened when they witness—and report—military crimes against civilians, such as using Palestinian children as human shields. Young boys stopped by Israeli soldiers have been beaten to death, and the desperately ill traveling by ambulance to the hospital turned back at Israeli checkpoints.[12] Omri Sharon, the son of Prime Minister Ariel Sharon, has stated quite candidly that "Any talk of a Palestinian state is a ruse . . ." and that Israel is "violating international agreements, but no one is saying anything. The United States is with us. . . ."[13] He is entirely correct. The United States is pouring billions of dollars into the Israeli killing machine, and no one says, "For God's sake, stop!"

The Institute for Advanced Strategic and Political Studies, a Jerusalem-based think tank with an office in Washington, D.C., produced a report in 1996 for the newly elected Israeli

prime minister, Benjamin Netanyahu. The chief author of this
report was Richard Perle, who, because of his murky business
dealings with powerful Middle Eastern businesses, was forced
to step down as chair of the Pentagon's Defense Policy Board.
Despite questions regarding a conflict of interest Perle remained
as a member of the Defense Policy Board at the request of the
Secretary of Defense Donald Rumsfeld.[14] The advice given to
Netanyahu by Perle and this right-wing think tank was to adopt
a policy of "peace through strength" by engaging in military
strikes against Syria and the Hezbollah. The report pushed for
removing Saddam Hussein from power as "an important Israeli
strategic objective in its own right."[15]

As Rashid Khalidi points out,

> Equally noteworthy in the 1996 report is the perception
> of a complete identity of Israeli and American interests in
> the Middle East. . . . The similarity of tone between these
> recommendations and the Bush administration's global
> strategy is obvious. What should also be obvious is that
> these prescriptions constitute the template for current
> American strategy toward the Middle East generally and
> Iraq in particular, and for a new form of American hege-
> mony over the region in collaboration with Israel.[16]

In *The Price of Loyalty,* Paul O'Neill describes a meeting of
the National Security Council in which President George W.
Bush said, "We are going to correct the imbalances of the previous administration on the Mideast conflict. We're going to
tilt it back toward Israel. And we're going to be consistent. . . .
I don't see much we can do over there at this point. I think it's
time to pull out of that situation." An incredulous Secretary of
State Colin Powell replied, "The consequence of that could be
dire, especially for the Palestinians." The president shrugged
and said, "Maybe that's the best way to get things back in bal-
ance. . . . Sometimes a show of strength by one side can really

clarify things."[17] Matters have indeed been clarified. It is clear that Israel may practice cruelty and barbarity with the full support and encouragement of the United States.

For Christians this is not a "political issue" as narrowly defined. It is a spiritual and religious issue. We are called to live lives of justice in which we champion the cause of the vulnerable and demonstrate solidarity with the oppressed. We are called to lives of divine compassion in which we ask not "Who is my neighbor?" but "Whose neighbor can I be?" We are called to do good to all people, beginning with the "household of faith" (Galatians 6:10). This most certainly includes our suffering Palestinian Christian brothers and sisters and their Muslim neighbors in Gaza and the West Bank.

Although a Hindu, Mahatma Gandhi saw love as the basic law of our being, and the only authentic force of universal and practical application.[18] In this insight Gandhi was radically Christian. One of the intriguing things about him is that by reading the New Testament and discovering Christ and his teaching, Gandhi deepened his own Hindu traditions.[19]

In developing the nonviolent resistance movement in India Gandhi coined the term *satyagraha,* which literally means "holding to the truth" or "insistence upon the truth." "Satya-" comes from the Sanskrit word for "being" and means both "truth" and "essence." *Satyagraha* connotes creative force, or power. It is, therefore, "soul force." He sometimes translated it into English as "love force" and "truth force."[20] What Gandhi believed was that by following the way of *satyagraha* he was following the way of Christ. He said, "Jesus lived and died in vain if he did not teach us to regulate the whole of life by the eternal law of love."[21]

This is fundamental Christian doctrine. To become a disciple of Christ is to become a *satyagrahi.* It is to be in conscious communion with the One who is Love and Truth. It is to take the vow of truth. It is to be at one with the supernatural power of truth. Saint Paul urges us to be people who "speak the truth in love" (Ephesians 4:25), or, more literally, to become people who are "*truthing* one another in love." That is, simply, being truth. This is the only way that there will ever be peace in the Middle East—for us to insist on truth, and to follow the Master in the company of the *satyagrahi*. What counts in the end—and Jesus was absolutely clear in his teaching about this—is not what we profess but the reality of what we are in the essence of our being. Hell's abyss and heaven's grace are in us, "What we elect and want we have in any place."

Notes

All URLs referenced in these notes were live as of the time of publication.

Epigraph

1. Dale W. Brown, *Biblical Pacifism: A Peace Church Perspective* (Elgin, Ill.: Brethren Press, 1968).

Introduction

1. H. A. Reinhold, ed. *The Soul Afire* (New York: Pantheon Books, 1944), 26.

2. E. Stanley Jones, *The Way* (Nashville: Stone and Pierce, 1946), 1.

3. Ibid.

4. John Howard Yoder, *What Would You Do? A Serious Answer to a Standard Question* (Scottdale, Penn.: Herald Press, 1983).

5. Samuel Taylor Coleridge, "The Rime of the Ancient Mariner," in *The Portable Coleridge,* ed. I. A. Richards (New York: Viking Penguin Press, 1956), 80–105.

6. Henri J. M. Nouwen, *The Path of Peace* (New York: Crossroad Publishing, 1995), 19–20.

Chapter 1

1. Neil Diamond, "The Good Lord Loves You," from *September Morn: Record,* prod. Bob Gaudio (New York: CBS, Inc., 1979). Manufactured by Columbia Records.

2. Evelyn Hong, "The US–UN Sanctions on Iraq—Globalisation and

the Impact on Health—A Third World View," *People's Health Movement,* August 2000, http://www.phmovement.org/pubs/issuepapers/hong20 .html.

3. Donna Abu-Nasr, "Kid's Plight Shakes GI's Faith," *The Denver Post,* 24 June 2003, 2A.

4. Barbara Brown Taylor, "The Luminous Web," *The Christian Century,* 2–9 June 1999, 616.

5. Ibid., 614, 618.

6. Ibid., 619.

7. Cynthia Bourgeault, *Mystical Hope: Trusting in the Mercy of God* (Cambridge, Mass.: Cowley Publications, 2001), 35–36.

8. Henri J. M. Nouwen, *The Path of Peace* (New York: Crossroad Publishing, 1995), 45–46.

9. "Military Toxic Pollution: A Threat to Public Health and the Environment," *Be Safe Platform: Coordinated by the Center for Health, Environment and Justice* (2004): 1–5, http://www.besafenet.com/ Military%20Toxics.htm; Jeffery St. Clair, "The Military's Toxic Time-bombs: No One Is Cleaning Up the Pentagon's Hazardous Messes," *In These Times,* 28 May 2001, 1–3, www.inthesetimes.com/site/main/ article/the_militarys_toxic_timebombs.

10. "Communities in the Line of Fire: The Environmental, Cul-tural, and Human Health Impacts of Military Munitions and Firing Ranges," *Prepared by the Military Toxics Project,* June 2002, http:// www.miltoxproj.org/cm_report.htm.

11. Ibid.

12. Ibid.

13. Bland, "The Military and Nuclear Pollution," 4–5.

14. Arundhati Roy, *War Talk* (Cambridge, Mass.: South End Press, 2003), 65.

15. "Current Hunger and Poverty Statistics," *America's Second Harvest: Creating a Hunger Free America* (2002): 1–2, http://www.secondharvest .org/site_content.asp?s=59 See also "Make Change," *Grassroots,* August 2004, http://www.homeless.org/do/Home; Susan Brown, "Millions Still Face Homelessness in a Booming Economy," *Urban Institute: A Nonpartisan Economic and Secular Policy Research Organization* (1 February 2000): 1–2, http://www.urban.org/Template.cfm?Section =PressReleases&NavMenuID=4& PublicationI...; "Background and Statistics: Detailed Statistics and Analysis of Homelessness in the

U.S.," *National Alliance to End Homelessness,* 2003, http://www
.endhomelessness.org/back/; "Hunger and the Elderly," *Apples for Health,*
4 February 2000, http://www.applesforhealth.com/hungerelder1.html;
"Hunger and Food Insecurity Among the Elderly," *Food Security Center: The Heller Graduate School for Social Policy and Management,
Brandeis University* (February 2003): 1–11, www.centeronhunger.org/
pdf/Elderly.pdf; Anuradha Mittal, "Hunger in America," *Common Dreams News Center,* 10 December 2004, 1–2, http://www
.commondreams.org/views04/1210-22.htm; Sara Fass and Nancy K.
Cauthen, "Who Are America's Poor Children?" *National Center for
Children in Poverty: Columbia University School of Public Health*
(September 2005): 1–3, http://www.nccp.org/pub_cpt05b.html; Ayana
Douglas-Hall and Heather Koball, "Basic Facts about Low Income
Children," *National Center for Children in Poverty: Columbia University School of Public Health* (July 2005): 1–3, http://www.nccp
.org/pub_lic05.html; "Homelessness and Poverty in America," *National Law Center on Homelessness and Poverty* (December 2004): 1–2,
http://www.nlchp.org?FA%5FHAP1A/2004; Jonathan Alter, "Poverty
in America: The Truths That Katrina Laid Bare," *Newsweek Magazine*
156, no. 12 (September 19, 2005): 42–48.

16. Marie Panton, "Crisis in Health Care," *Episcopal Life* (July–August
2004): 1, 6.

17. Martha Austin, "Hospitals Turn Away Ill, Injured," *The Denver
Post,* 29 June 2003, 1A, 2A.

18. "Guns and Butter: A Green Party Review of Your Tax Dollars at
Work," *The Green Party of the United States,* 30 June 2003, http://www
.gp.org/articles/gunsnbutter.shtml; Anuradha Mittal, "Hunger in
America," *Common Dreams News Center,* 10 December 2004, http://
www.commondreams.org/views04/1210-22.htm.

19. Ibid.

20. Jim Efstathiou, "Firm's Till Fat with Iraq Money," *Bakersfield
Californian,* 30 May 2003, C1–C2. See also Mark Gongloff, "Iraq Rebuilding Contracts Awarded," *CNN Money,* 25 March 2003, http://
money.cnn.com/2003/03/25/news/companies/war_contracts/; Pratrap
Chatterjee, "Bechtel Wins Iraq War Contracts," *CorpWatch.org,* 24 April
2003, http://www.corpwatch.org/article.php?id=6532 ; "Guns and Butter," 1–3.

21. Pratrap Chatterjee, "Halliburton Makes a Killing on Iraq War,"

CorpWatch, 20 March 2003, 1–4, http:www.corpwatch.org/article.php ?id=6008.

22. Chatterjee, "Bechtel Wins Iraq War Contracts."

23. "Report on Defense Contractor to the Defense Policy Board," *Citizen Works,* 3 April 2003, 1, http://www.citizenworks.org/corp/ pentagon.php. See also "Guns and Butter"; Walter F. Roche Jr. and Ken Silverstein, "Advocates of War Now Profit From Iraq's Reconstruction," *Los Angeles Times,* 14 July 2004, A1, A8–A9.

24. "President Bush's Proposed FY Budget Hurts: Bush's 'Leave No Millionaire Behind' Tax Giveaways Undermine Vital Services," *American Federation of State, County, and Municipal Employees,* 2003, www.afscme.org/action/bushfy04.pdf.

25. Hannah Rosenthal, "Our Unfinished 40-Year War: Confronting Poverty, an Initiative of the Jewish Council for Public Affairs," *Jewish Public Affairs,* 23 January 2004, www.e-guana.net/organizations/org/ bushbudget2-5-04.doc.

26. James Horney, Joel Friedman, Richard Kogan, and Issac Shapiro, "Assessing the Budget Proposal Adopted by the Senate," *Center on Budget and Policy Priorities,* 1 April 2005, 1–4, http://www .cbpp.org/3-23-05bud.htm. See also Mike Allen and Peter Baker, "$2.5 Trillion Budget Plan Cuts Many Programs," *Washington Post,* 7 February 2005, A01.

27. Horney et al., "Assessing the Budget Proposal Adopted by the Senate."

28. Roy, *War Talk,* 70.

29. Jennie Emiko Kuida, "Why You Should Boycott Disney," *Jenni/ Tony Homepage* (originally Published in *The Rafu Shimpo*), 24 June 1997, http://www.kuidaosumi.com/Jkwriting/disney.html.

30. David Moberg, "Laws of Empire," *In These Times,* 7 July 2003, http://www.inthesetimes.com/comments.php?id=244_0_3_0_C.

31. Roy, *War Talk,* 69.

32. Peronet Despeignes, "Census: Poverty Rose by Million: Uninsured Rate also Escalates," *USA Today,* 27–29 August 2004, 1A.

33. Noam Chomsky, *On Power and Ideology: The Managua Lectures* (Cambridge, Mass.: South End Press, 1987), 75.

34. John MacQuarrie, *The Concept of Peace* (New York: Harper & Row, 1973), 63.

35. Kenneth S. Wuest, *Wuest's Word Studies: Romans in the Greek New Testament for the English Reader* (Grand Rapids, Mich.: William B. Eerdmans, 1955), 213–14.

36. S. Craig Glickman, *A Song for Lovers* (Downers Grove, Ill.: Inter-Varsity Press, 1980), 17, 30.

37. Ethelbert Stauffer, *"agapao," Theological Dictionary of the New Testament,* vol. 1, ed. Gerhard Kittel and Geoffrey W. Bromiley, trans. Geoffrey W. Bromiley (Grand Rapids, Mich.: William B. Eerdmans, 1964), 24.

38. Robinson Jeffers, "Nova," in *The Selected Poetry of Robinson Jeffers,* ed. Tim Hunt (Stanford, Calif.: Stanford University Press, 2001), 520–21.

39. Stauffer, *"agapao,"* 24.

40. *Disciples of Christ in Community: Presenter's Manual,* session 12 (Sewanee, Tenn.: The University of the South, 1999), 1–4.

41. Gerald G. May, *Will and Spirit: A Contemplative Psychology* (San Francisco: Harper & Row, 1982), 171.

42. Ibid.

Chapter 2

1. M. Scott Peck, *People of the Lie: The Hope for Healing Human Evil* (New York: Simon and Schuster, 1983), 69–84.

2. Ibid., 78.

3. Ibid.

4. Ibid., 83.

5. Ibid., 76.

6. Ibid., 73.

7. Ibid., 74.

8. Ibid., 69.

9. Dietrich Bonhoeffer, *No Rusty Swords: Letters, Lectures, and Notes from the Collected Works of Dietrich Bonhoeffer,* ed. Edwin H. Robertson, trans. Edwin H. Robertson and John Bowden (New York: Harper & Row, 1965), 20–23, 221. See also Victoria Barnett. "Dietrich Bonhoeffer," *United States Holocaust Memorial Museum,* B1–B5, http://www.ushmm.org/bonhoeffer/b1.htm; John W. de Gruchy, ed., *The Cambridge Companion of Dietrich Bonhoeffer* (Cambridge: Cambridge University Press, 1999), 34–39, 246–65.

10. Wayne Whitson Floyd Jr., "Theologian Executed on Order from Hitler," *Christian History Institute,* no. 63 (2004), http://chi.gospelcom.net/GLIMPSEF/Glimpses/glmps063.shtml.

11. Dietrich Bonhoeffer, *The Cost of Discipleship* (New York: The Macmillan Company, 1966), 133–36.

12. Susan Clemmer Steiner, *Joining the Army That Sheds No Blood* (Kitchener, Ont.: Herald Press, 1982), 80–81. See also Clayborne Carson, ed., *The Autobiography of Martin Luther King, Jr.* (New York: Warner Books, 1998), 50–82.

13. Steiner, *Joining the Army That Sheds No Blood,* 80–81. See also Marshall Frady, *Martin Luther King, Jr.* (New York: Viking Press, 2002), 46–47.

14. Dave Jackson and Neta Jackson, *Hero Tales,* vol. 2 (Minneapolis: Bethany House Publishers, 1997), 69–79.

15. Anne Coomes, *The Authorized Biography of Festo Kivengere* (Eastbourne, U.K.: Monarch Publications, 1990), 286, 293, 297, 302–4, 316–17. See also Jill Briscoe, *The Man Who Would Not Hate: The Story of Festo Kivengere* (Waco, Tex.: Word Publishing, 1991), 32–38.

16. Coomes, *The Authorized Biography of Festo Kivengere,* 286.

17. Briscoe, *The Man Who Would Not Hate,* 43–46. See also Frederick Quinn, *African Saints: Saints, Martyrs, and Holy People from the Continent of Africa* (New York: Crossroad, 2002), 117–18.

18. Coomes, *The Authorized Biography of Festo Kivengere,* 345. See also Briscoe, *The Man Who Would Not Hate,* 42.

19. Briscoe, *The Man Who Would Not Hate,* 39–49

20. Ibid., 33–35.

21. Coomes, *The Authorized Biography of Festo Kivengere,* 415–41.

22. Richard Rohr, *The Path of Non-Violence* (audiocassette) (Bend, Ore.: Spirit Records, 1998). See also Walter Wink, *Jesus and Nonviolence: A Third Way.* Facets (Minneapolis: Fortress Press, 2003).

23. Ibid. See also Richard Rohr, *Job and the Mystery of Suffering: Spiritual Reflections* (New York: Crossroad, 1996), 181; Henri J. M. Nouwen, *Letters to Marc About Jesus* (New York: Harper & Row, 1988), 30–33.

24. Jeanette Petrie, dir. and prod., "Mother Teresa," (A Today Home Entertainment Video Presentation, 1986).

25. Johannes Baptiste Metz, *Poverty of Spirit,* trans. John Drury (New York: Paulist Press, 1968), 37–38.

26. Ibid., 40.

27. Laurence Shames and Peter Barton, *Not Fade Away: A Short Life Well Lived* (New York: HarperPerennial, 2004), 100.

28. William A. Barry, sj, *Paying Attention to God: Discernment in Prayer* (Notre Dame, Ind.: Ave Maria Press, 1990), 29.

29. Robert Coles, "The Inexplicable Prayers of Ruby Bridges," *Christianity Today,* 9 August 1985, 17–20.

30. Ibid., 20.

31. Ibid.

32. Dianna Ortiz with Patricia Davis, *The Blindfold's Eyes: My Journey from Torture to Truth* (Maryknoll, N.Y.: Orbis Books, 2002).

33. Lee Hockstader and Douglas Farah, "6 Priests, 2 Others Slain in San Salvador," *Washington Post Foreign Service,* 17 November 1989, A1.

34. Noam Chomsky, *On Power and Ideology: The Managua Lectures,* (Cambridge, Mass.: South End Press, 1987), 59–60.

35. Halford E. Luccock, *Christianity and the Individual in a World of Crowds* (Nashville: Cokesbury Press, 1937), 38.

36. Robert Raines, *To Kiss the Joy* (Waco, Tex.: Word Books, 1973), 29.

37. Gerald G. May, *Will and Spirit: A Contemplative Psychology* (San Francisco: Harper & Row, 1982), 278.

38. Ibid., 279.

39. Lao Tsu, *Tao Te Ching.* Trans. Gia-Fu Feng and Jane English (New York: Knopf, 1972), chap. 47.

40. May, *Will and Spirit,* 280.

41. Ibid.

42. Dan R. Stiver and Daniel O. Aleshire, "Mapping the Spiritual Journey," in *Becoming Christian: Dimensions of Spiritual Formation,* ed. Bill J. Leonard (Louisville, Ky.: Westminster John Knox Press, 1990), 20–21.

43. Norvene Vest, *Preferring Christ: A Devotional Commentary and Workbook on the Rule of St. Benedict* (Harrisburg, Pa.: Morehouse Publishers, 2004), 7.

44. Charles Mortimer Guilbert (Custodian of the Standard Book of Common Prayer), *The Book of Common Prayer and Administration of the Sacraments and Other Rites and Ceremonies of the Church Together with the Psalter of psalms of David According to the use of the Episcopal Church* (New York: Church Publishing, Inc., 1979), 855.

Chapter 3

1. Abraham Lincoln, "Second Inaugural Address: March 4, 1865," House Document 91–142, in *Inaugural Addresses of the Presidents of the United States: From George Washington 1789 to Richard Millhouse Nixon 1969,* 91st Cong., 1st sess. (Washington, D.C.: GPO, 1969), 127–28.

2. Bruce Canto, *The Civil War* (Boston: Houghton Mifflin Company, 1960), 156–71. See also Pauline Maier, Merritt Roe Smith, Alexander Keyssar, and Daniel Kevles, *Inventing America: A History of the United States* (New York: W. W. Norton and Company, 2003), 580–82.

3. Patrick Kelly, "Does God Support Democracy? The President's Justification for War in Iraq Demands Scrutiny," *National Catholic Reporter* (February 4, 2005): http://www.natcath.com/NCR_Online/archives2/2005a/020405/020405x.php; Jason Hall, "Panel: War with Iraq Justified according to Biblical Standard," *Free Republic* (February 27, 2003): http://www.freerepublic.com/focus/news/853405/posts; "Americans Seek Divine Providence in Iraq War," *SpaceWar.com,* 30 March 2003, http://www.spacewar.com/2003-a/030330183620.ljsrvivl.html.

4. Joseph Carter Swaim, *War, Peace, and the Bible* (Maryknoll, N.Y.: Orbis Books, 1982), 7.

5. Dale W. Brown, *Biblical Pacifism: A Peace Church Perspective* (Elgin, Ill.: Brethren Press, 1986), 66.

6. Swaim, *War, Peace, and the Bible,* 10–14.

7. D. W. Brown, *Biblical Pacifism,* 66–67.

8. Abraham Joshua Heschel, *The Prophets* (New York: Harper & Row, 1962), 210.

9. Ibid., 198.

10. Swaim, *War, Peace, and the Bible,* 11.

11. Alfred Lord Tennyson, "Flower in the Crannied Wall," in *Burning Bright: An Anthology of Sacred Poetry,* ed. Patricia Hampl (New York: Ballentine Books, 1995), 13.

12. Dee Brown, *Bury My Heart at Wounded Knee: An Indian History of the American West* (New York: Holt, Rinehart & Winston, 1971), 7–8.

13. Ibid., 1. See also Frederick Turner, ed., *Geronimo: His Own Story as Told to S. M. Barrett* (New York: Meridian Books, 1996), 5–14.

14. Peter d'Errico (web site author), "Jeffrey Amherst and Smallpox Blankets: Amherst's Letters Discussing Germ Warfare against American Indians," *NativeWeb.org*, http://www.nativeweb.org/pages/legal/amherst/lord_jeff.html

15. Thomas Merton, *Essential Writings*. Ed. Christine M. Bochen (Maryknoll, N.Y.: Orbis Books, 2000), 13–14.

16. Maier et al., *Inventing America*, 436.

17. Ibid., 443–46.

18. J. Buschini, "The Spanish-American War: Remember the *Maine*," *Small Planet.com* 2000, http://www.smplanet.com/imperialism/remember.html.

19. Ibid.

20. Maier et al., *Inventing America*, 668–72.

21. Ibid., 671.

22. Ibid., 669–71.

23. Ibid., 719. See also Jill E. Julin, Meredith L. Berg, and Donita R. McWilliams, "The Sinking of the *Lusitania*," *Northpark University: United States of America Chronolgy*, 26 January 2003, 1–2, http://campus.northpark.edu/history/WebChron/USA/Lusitania.CP.html.

24. Wilbur H. Morrison, *Twentieth Century American Wars* (New York: Hippocrene Books, 1993), 87.

25. Glenn Hasted, "The Lend Lease Act," *Encyclopedia of American Foreign Policy* (New York: Facts on File, Inc., 2004), 292–93.

26. "General Curtis Emerson LeMay," *The Nuclear Age Peace Foundation*, 1–20, http://www.nuclearfiles.org/menu/library/biographies/bio_lemay-curtis.htm. See also Mickey Z, "On the Winning Side: Curtis LeMay's Brand of Hell," *Counter Punch* (5 March 2003): 1, http://www.counterpunch.org/mickey0305203.html.

27. Douglass Cassel, "Guatemala: Will Democracy Rise From the Dead?" *Center for International Human Rights* (29 June 1994): 1–2, http://www.law.northwestern.edu/depts/clinic/ihr/display_details .cfm?ID=26&document_t...; See also "Chile Remembers 25 Years Since U.S. Backed Coup," *Democracy Now* (11 September 1998): 1–3, http://www.democracynow.org/articles.pl?sid=03/04/07/0346254; "US 'Undermined Chile's Democracy,'" *BBC News*, 14 November 2000, 1–3, file://C:\DOCUME~1\Chery\LOCALS~1\Temp\DJZ8GJGF.htm.

28. David Barsamian, "Secrets, Lies and Democracy: Interview

with Noam Chomsky," *Third World Traveler* (11 December 2004): 1–3, http://www.thirdworldtraveler.com/Chomsky/SecretsLies_Chile _Chom.html.

29. Ibid.

30. Seymour M. Hersh, *The Price of Power: Kissinger in the Nixon White House* (New York: Summit Books, 1983), 259. See also Amit Sen Gupta, "Peddling Poison," *People's Democracy* 27 no. 33 (17 August 2003): 1–4, http://pd.cpim.org/2003/0817/08172003_snd.hrm.

31. Noam Chomsky, *On Power and Ideology: The Managua Lectures* (Cambridge, Mass.: South End Press, 1987), 28, 35. See also Barsamian, "Secrets, Lies, and Democracy," 2.

32. Barsamian, "Secrets, Lies and Democracy," 2.

33. Ibid.

34. Ibid.

35. Ibid., 1.

36. Edward S. Herman, "How the Pitbull Manages His Poodles," *Z Magazine Online* 16, no. 1 (January 2003): 1–4, http://zmagsite.zmag .org/Jan2003/hermanprint0103.shtml. See also Edward S. Herman, "Threat Inflation: Going After Hapless Countries," *Z Magazine Online* 16, no. 3 (March 2003): 2–3, http://www.thirdworldtraveler.com/ Propaganda/Threat_Inflation.html.

37. "A 'Killing Field' in the Americas: US Policy in Guatemala," *Third World Traveler*, 1–8, http://www.thirdworldtraveler.com/US _ThirdWorld/US_Guat.html.

38. Ibid., 2.

39. "Multinational Companies: United Fruit Co, Chiquita," *Virtual Truth Commission*, 1–3, http://www.geocities.com/~virtualtruth/ Chiquita.htm.

40. David Batstone, "The 'Democracy Option' Disappears in Iraq," *Sojourners*, January 2005, http://www.sojo.net/index.cfm ?action=sojomail.display&issue=050119#3.

41. Arundhati Roy, *War Talk* (Cambridge, Mass.: South End Press, 2003), 89–90.

42. Heschel, *The Prophets*, 204.

43. Bishop Don Helder Camara, "From Saint to Communist," LeiterReports.com, July 2004, http://www.leiterreports.typepad.com/ blog/2004/07/from_saint_to_c.html.

44. Tom Kim, "The Gulf of Tonkin Incident," *United States of America Chronology*, North Park University, 17 December 1999, 1–2, http://campus.northpark.edu/history/WebChron/USA/GulfTonkin .CP.html.

45. John Stauber and Sheldon Rampton, "How Public Relations Sold the Gulf War to the U.S.," *Hartford Web Publishing*, 29 August 1996, 1–2, http://www.hartford-hwp.com/archives/51/076.html.

46. Ibid.

47. Scott Peterson, "In War, Some Facts Less Factual," *Christian Science Monitor*, 6 September 2002, 1–6, http://www.csmonitor.com/ 2002/0906/p01s02-wosc.html.

48. Rashid Khalidi, *Resurrecting Empire: Western Footprints and America's Perilous Path in the Middle East* (Boston: Beacon Press, 2004), 36.

49. Richard Rohr, *Job and the Mystery of Suffering* (New York: Crossroad Publishing Company, 2002), 168.

50. Coretta Scott King, "The Meaning of the Martin Luther King, Jr. Holiday," The King Center, 2004, 1–6, http://thekingcenter.org/ holiday/index.asp. See also James Melvin Washington, ed,. *A Testament of Hope: The Essential Writings of Martin Luther King, Jr.* (San Francisco: Harper & Row, 1986), 231–44, 253–58, 268–78, 313–28, 497–517.

51. Marcus J. Borg, *The Heart of Christianity: Rediscovering the Life of Faith* (San Francisco: HarperSanFrancisco, 2003), 136–37.

52. Ibid., 137.

53. Ibid.

54. Ibid.

55. Borg, *The Heart of Christianity*, 136. See also Philippians 3:20.

Chapter 4

1. Diane Knippers, "Coming to Terms with War: Christians Appropriately Support Just War," *Episcopal Life* (July–August 2002): 28.

2. Ibid.

3. Lars Erika, "William Tecumseh Sherman," *Military Quotes*, November 2002, http://www.military-quotes.com; See also "William Tecumseh Sherman: War Is Hell," *Thoughts Worth Thinking*, http:// www.rjgeib.com/thoughts/sherman/sherman.html.

4. W. James Antle III, "Congress Must Declare Iraq War,"

Free Republic, September 2002, http://www.freerepublic.com/focus/news/743697/posts.

5. Pauline Maier, Merrit Rose Smith, Alexander Keyssar, and Daniel J. Kevles, *Inventing America: A History of the United States* (New York: W. W. Norton Company, 2003), 882. See also John Dean, "Findlaw Forum: President Needs Congressional Approval to Declare War on Iraq" *CNN Law Center,* 30 August 2002, http://www.cnn.com/2002/LAW/08/columns/fl.dean.warpowers/.

6. Maier et al., *Inventing America,* 981. See also Dean, "Findlaw Forum: President Needs Congressional Approval to Declare War on Iraq," 1–8.

7. Noam Chomsky, "Imperial Presidency," *Z Magazine* 18, no. 2 (February 2005): 37–45.

8. Gene Healy, "War with Iraq: Who Decides?" *Cato Institute,* 26 February 2002, http://www.cato.org/dailys/02-26-02.html.

9. Stephen R. Shalom, "Iraq: War and Democracy," *Z Magazine Online,* April 2003, http://Zmagsite.zmag.org/Apr2003/shalom0403.html.

10. Ibid.

11. Ibid.

12. "Iraq War Illegal, says Annan," *BBC News: UK Edition,* 16 September 2004, http://news.bbc.co.uk/1/hi/world/middle_east/3661134.stm.

13. Nicolas J. S. Davies, "The Crime of War: From Nuremberg to Fallujah," *Z Magazine* 18, no.2 (February 2005): 33–36.

14. Francis Schaffer, *Genesis in Space and Time: The Flow of Biblical History* (Downers Grove, Ill.: InterVarsity Press, 1972), 52–52.

15. Tucker Carlson, "Devil May Care," *Talk Magazine* (September 1999): 106. Posted on *DangerousCitizen.com,* 9 May 2003, http://www.dangerouscitizen.com/Photo+Gallery/568.aspx.

16. "Alberto Gonzales: A Record of Injustice," *Center for American Progress,* 12 November 2004, http://www.americanprogress.org/site/pp.asp?c=biJRJ8OVF&b=246536.

17. Ibid.

18. "Osama's 'Head on Dry Ice,'" *Dawn Internet Edition,* 4 May 2005, http://www.Dawn.com/2005/05/04/int16.htm.

19. Matthew Engle, "Bush Reveals First Thought, 'There's One

Terrible Pilot'," *Guardian Unlimited,* 5 December 2001, http://www
.guardian.co.uk/september11/story/,0.11209,612354,00.html.

20. "Rumsfeld Responsible for Torture Report," Associated Press,
16 May 2004. Quoted in *ReligiousNewsBlog.com,* http://www.google
.com/search?hl=en&ie=ISO-8859-1&q=%93Rumsfeld+Responsible
+for+Torture+Report%94. See also Peter Eisler and Tom Squitieri,
"Red Cross Report Describes Systematic Abuse in Iraq," *USA Today,*
10 May 2004, http:www.usatoday.com/news/world/iraq/2004-05-10
-redcross_x.htm.

21. Bruce Jackson, "Bush Gets Testy About Torture," *CounterPunch
.com,* 14 June 2004, http://www.counterpunch.org/jackson06142004
.html.

22. See Luke 9:54–56.

23. Dick Meyer, "Rush: MPs Just 'Blowing off Steam,'" *CBSNews
.Com,* 6 May 2004, http://www.cbsnews.com/stories/2004/05/06/
opinion/meyer/main616021.shtml.

24. "CIA Flying Suspects to Torture?" *60 Minutes,* 6 March 2005,
http://www.cbsnewyork.com/topstories/topstories_story_065094819
.html.

25. Nee To-sheng, *What Shall This Man Do?* (Fort Washington,
Penn.: Christian Literature Crusade, reprinted 1972), 119, 121–22.

26. "Bush's Carrier Landing Another Big Lie," *RightWingLies.com,*
2 May 2003, http://www.rightwinglies.com/Bush%20Lies/carrier.htm.

27. Ron Suskind, *The Price of Loyalty: George W. Bush, the White
House, and the Education of Paul O'Neill* (New York: Simon and
Schuster, 2004), 147–48.

28. Ibid., 148–49.

29. Lao Tsu, *Tao Te Ching.* Ed. Gia-Fu Feng and Jane English (New
York: Random House Publishers, 1972), chap. 31.

30. Toby Keith, "Courtesy of the Red White and Blue (The Angry
American)," from *Unleashed,* prod. James Stroud and Toby Keith (Nash-
ville: SKG Music Nashville LLC, 2002). Manufactured by Dreamworks
Records Nashville.

31. The Bloodhound Gang, "Fire Water Burn," from *One Fierce Beer
Coaster,* prod. Jimmy Pop Ali (Los Angeles: Geffe Records, 1996).

32. Eugenio Zolli, *Before the Dawn: Autobiographical Reflections*
(New York: Sheed & Ward, 1954), 181.

33. Richard A. Clarke, *Against All Enemies: Inside America's War on Terror* (New York: Free Press, 2004), 265.

34. Ken Roth, "War in Iraq: Not a Humanitarian Intervention," *Human Rights Watch World Report*, January 2004, http://www.hrw .org/wr2k4/3.htm.

35. Ibid., 4.

36. Ibid., 5.

37. Chomsky, "Imperial Presidency," 38.

38. Roth, "War in Iraq: Not a Humanitarian Intervention," 8.

39. Ibid.

40. Emad Mekay, "War Launched to Protect Israel—Bush Adviser," *IPSNews.com*, 29 March 2004, http://www.ipsnews.net/interna.asp ?idnews=23083.

41. Ibid.

42. Ibid.

43. Ivan Eland, "US Foreign Policy: Question All Assumptions," *Skyhen.Org*, 18 January 2005, http://www.skyhen.org/AmericanEmpire/ us_foreign_policy_question_all_assumptions.php. See also Ted Galen Carpenter, "Democracy and War," review of *Death by Government* by R. J. Rummel in *Independent Review* (Winter 1998): 435–41, www .independent.org/pdf/tir/tir_02_3_carpenter.pdf.

44. Melvin Butch Hollowell and Len Niehoff, "Local Comment: To Even Consider Suppressing the Vote Shames a Democracy," *Detroit Free Press*, 27 July 2004, http://www.freep.com/voices/columnists/ eholl27_20040727.htm.

45. Charles Mortimer Guilbert (Custodian of the Standard Book of Common Prayer), *The Book of Common Prayer and Administration of the Sacraments and Other Rites and Ceremonies of the Church Together with the Psalter of psalms of David According to the use of the Episcopal Church* (New York: Church Publishing, Inc., 1979), 305.

46. Stephen Graham, "Lagging Development Means Afghanistan Could Fail Again, U.N. Warns," *Associated Press*, 21 February 2005, http://www.usatoday.com/news/world/2005-02-21-afghan-un_x.htm ?csp=36.

47. Stephen J. Hedges, "Military to Leave Saudi Arabia: US Moving Amid Strained Relations," *Chicago Tribune*, 30 April 2003, http://www. globalsecurity.org/org/news/2003/030430-psab01.htm.

48. *Fahrenheit 9/11*, DVD, directed by Michael Moore (Columbia TriStar, 2006).

49. William Clark, "Revisited—The Real Reasons for the Upcoming War with Iraq: A Macroeconomic and Geostrategic Analysis of the Unspoken Truth," *Rat Haus Reality*, January 2003 (revised March 2003), http://www.ratical.org/ratville/CAH/RRiraqWar.html.

50. Chomsky, "Imperial Presidency," 40.

51. Seymour M. Hersh, "A Case Not Closed, *The New Yorker*, 1 November 1993, posted 27 September 2002, http://www.newyorker.com/archive/content/?020930fr_archive02.

52. Arundhati Roy, *War Talk* (Cambridge, Mass.: South End Press, 2003), 52.

53. Mark Lawson, "Bring Out Your Dead," *Guardian Unlimited*, 24 April 2004, http://www.guardian.co.uk/story/0,3604,1202246,00.html.

54. Rashid Khalidi, *Resurrecting Empire: Western Footprints and America's Perilous Path in the Middle East* (Boston: Beacon Press, 2004): 49–55.

55. Suskind, *The Price of Loyalty*, 72–75.

56. "The Secret Downing Street Memo," *TimesOnline: The Sunday Times—Britain*, May 2005, 1–2, http://www.timesonline.couk/article/0,,2087-1593607,00.html.

57. Gregory W. Hamilton, "Preemptive Strike Doctrine: The Prophetic Unveiling of the World's Last Empire?" *Liberty Express Journal* (Summer 2003): 1–7, http://www.libertyexpress.org/content2003/Newsletter/Summer%202004/2-PreemptiveStrikeDoctrine.htm.

58. Ibid.

59. Chomsky, "Imperial Presidency," 41.

60. Neta C. Crawford, "The Best Defense: The Problem with Bush's 'Preemptive' War Doctrine," *Boston Review* (February–March 2003): 115, http://www.bostonreview.net/BR28.1/crawford.html.

61. Khalidi, *Resurrecting Empire*, 50–51. See also R. A. Clarke, *Against All Enemies*, 30.

62. R. A. Clarke, *Against All Enemies*, 30.

63. Ibid., 32.

64. Suskind. *The Price of Loyalty*, 73.

65. John H. Cushman Jr., "Panel Describes Long Weakening of Hussein Army," *New York Times,* 18 July 2004, 1, 8.

66. Suskind, *The Price of Loyalty,* 258.

67. Khalidi, *Resurrecting Empire,* 2–3.

68. R. A. Clarke, *Against All Enemies,* 266.

69. *The 9/11 Commission Report of the National Commission on Terrorist Attacks Upon the United States* (New York: W. W. Norton Company Ltd., 2004), 334–35, 559. See also Philip Shenon and Christopher Marquis, "Challenges Bush: A Chilling Chronology Rewrites the History of the Attacks," *New York Times,* 17 June 2004, A1, A15.

70. Dennis Bernstein, "Made in America," *San Francisco Bay Guardian,* 25 February 1998, 1–2, http://www.sfbg.com/News/32/21/Features/iraq.html.

71. Knippers, "Coming to Terms with War," 28.

72. Dana Bash, "White House Pressed on 'Mission Accomplished' Sign," *CNN.com,* 29 October 2003, http://www.cnn.com/2003/ALLPOLITICS/10/28/mission.accomplished/.

73. Claudia Wallis, "Hidden Scars of Battle," *Time* 164, no. 2 (12 July 2004): 35–36.

74. John Aloysius Farrell, "Deaths Mounting as Is Indifference," *Denver Post,* 8 August 2004, 25A.

75. "War Comes Home," *Christian Century* 121, no. 11 (1 June 2004): 5.

76. "A Year after Iraq War: Mistrust of America in Europe Even Higher, Muslim Anger Persists," *Pew Research Center,* 16 March 2004, http://people-press.org/reports/display.php3?ReportID=206.

77. Elise Labott, "U.S. Raises Figures for 2003 Terrorist Attacks," *CNN.com,* 22 June 2004, http://cnn.com/2004/ALLPOLITICS/06/22/powell.terror.

78. R. A. Clarke, *Against All Enemies,* 267.

79. James Whorton, "Radical Islam: The Cycle of History Repeats Itself," *WorldTribune.com,* 7 January 2003, http://worldtribune.com/worldtribune/Archives/arch-05.html.

80. Henry David Thoreau, *Walden; or Life in the Woods* (New York: Holt Rinehart and Winston, 1965), 267–68.

81. Paul Tillich, *Dynamics of Faith* (New York: Harper & Row, 1957): 11–12.

82. Barbara Bedway, "Why AP Counted Civilian Deaths in Iraq,"

Editor & Publisher, 24 June 2003, 1–2, http://www.editorandpublisher. com/eandp/news/article_display.jsp?vnu_content_id=1920081.

83. Lawson, "Bring Out Your Dead."

84. "Allies Deliberately Poisoned Public Water Supply in Gulf War," *The Sunday Herald,* 17 September 2000, http://www.sundayherald.com/ print10837.

85. "Caught in the Crossfire," *Christian Century* 119, no. 22 (23 October–5 November 2002): 5.

86. Eric Schmitt and Thom Shanker, "Rumsfeld Issued an Order to Hide Detainee in Iraq; Kept Him from Red Cross," *New York Times,* 17 June 2004, A1, A8, http://www.nytimes.com/2004/06/17/politics/ 17abuse.html. See also "Rumsfeld 'Backed Prison Abuse,'" *BBC News World Edition,* 29 August 2004, http://news.bbc.co.uk/2/hi/ americas/3718513.stm; Robert Burns, "Report: Rumsfeld, Senior Pentagon Officials Share Blame for Prisoner Abuse Scandal," *SFGate.com,* 24 August 2004, http://www.sfgate.com/cgi-bin/article.cgi?f=/news/ archive/2004/08/24/national1041EDT0518.DTL.

87. Alex Moseley, "Just War Theory," *Internet Encyclopedia of Philosophy,* http://www.utm.edu/research/iep/j/justwar.htm.

88. Khalidi, *Resurrecting Empire,* 175.

89. Kathleen Norris, *Dakota: A Spiritual Geography* (New York: Houghton Mifflin Company, 1983), 97–98.

Chapter 5

1. John Howard Yoder, *What Would You Do? A Serious Answer to a Standard Question* (Scottdale, Penn.: Herald Press, 1983), 14.

2. Ibid., 14.

3. Joseph Carter Swaim, *War, Peace, and the Bible* (Maryknoll, N.Y.: Orbis Books, 1982), 38.

4. Ibid., 16.

5. Ibid., 18.

6. Ibid., 18.

7. Reinhold Niebuhr, quoted in Yoder, *What Would You Do?* 18.

8. Yoder, *What Would You Do?* 19.

9. Ibid.

10. Ibid.

11. Ibid., 20.

12. Ibid.

13. Ibid., 21.

14. Ibid., 24.

15. Ibid., 26.

16. *Lesser Feasts and Fasts, 1997: Together with the Fixed Holy Days* (New York: Church Publishing Incorporated, 1998), 326–27.

17. Yoder, *What Would You Do?* 27.

18. Ibid., 28.

19. Ruth Fry *(Victories Without Violence),* quoted in Yoder, *What Would You Do?* 87–95.

20. Yoder, *What Would You Do?* 29.

21. Ibid., 34.

22. Ibid., 30.

23. Ibid.

24. Ibid., 30–32.

25. Ibid., 37.

26. Gerard Manley Hopkins, *"O Deus Ego Amo Te"* (attributed to St. Francis Xavier). In *Spiritual Direction and the Encounter with God: A Theological Inquiry,* William A. Barry, s.j. (New York: Paulist Press, 1992), 5. See also F. L. Cross and E. A. Livingston, eds., "Francis Xavier, St. (1506–52)," *The Oxford Dictionary of the Christian Church* (Oxford: Oxford University Press, 1974).

28. Yoder, *What Would You Do?* 38.

29. T. S. Eliot, *East Coker in Four Quartets: The Centenary Edition* (San Diego: Harcourt Brace Jovanovich Publishers, 1943, 1971), 28.

30. Yoder, *What Would You Do?* 39.

31. Ibid.

32. Alan Richardson, ed., *A Theological Wordbook of the Bible* (New York: Macmillan Publishers, 1950), 160–61.

33. Yoder, *What Would You Do?* 40.

34. Ibid.

35. Viktor E. Frankl, *Man's Search for Meaning.* Trans., Ilse Lasch (New York: Simon and Schuster, 1962), 132.

36. Ibid., 133–34.

37. Yoder, *What Would You Do?* 40.

38. Richard Stilgoe and Andrew Hart (book and lyrics), *The Phantom of the Opera.* Based on the novel *Le Fantôme de l'Opéra* by

Gaston Leroux. See http://www.theatre-musical.com/phantom/libretto .html.

39. Ibid.

40. Ibid., 41.

41. Ibid., 41–42.

Epilogue

1. "Robert Francis Kennedy Quotes," *ThinkExist.com,* http://www .thinkexist.com/English/Author/x/Author_4453_1.htm.

2. Viktor E. Frankl, *Man's Search for Ultimate Meaning* (New York: Basic Books, 2000), 40.

3. Marcus J. Borg, *The God We Never Knew: Beyond Dogmatic Religion to a More Authentic Contemporary Faith* (San Francisco: HarperSanFrancisco, 1997), 152.

4. Ibid., 150; Reinhold Niebuhr, quoted in ibid., 150.

5. "A Prayer Attributed to Saint Francis," in *The Book of Common Prayer and Administration of the Sacraments and Other Rites and Ceremonies of the Church Together with the Psalter of psalms of David According to the use of the Episcopal Church,* Charles Mortimer Guilbert (Custodian of the Standard Book of Common Prayer) (New York: Church Publishing, Inc., 1979), 833.

6. James W. Fowler, *Stages of Faith: The Psychology of Human Development and the Quest for Meaning* (San Francisco: Harper & Row, 1981), 201.

7. Frankl, *Man's Search for Ultimate Meaning,* 42.

8. Christian Maurer, *Theological Dictionary of the New Testament,* vol. 7. Ed. Gerhard Kittel and Gerhard Friedrich, trans. Geoffrey W. Bromiley (Grand Rapids, Mich.: Wm. B. Eerdmans Publishing Company, 1971), 908.

9. Frankl, *Man's Search for Ultimate Meaning,* 64.

10. Gerald G. May, *Will and Spirit: A Contemplative Psychology* (San Francisco: Harper & Row Publishers, 1983), 25.

11. Ibid.

12. David Steindl-Rast, *Gratefulness, the Heart of Prayer: An Approach to Life in Fullness* (New York: Paulist Press, 1984), 62.

13. See also 1 Chronicles 28:1–21 and Hebrews 9:23–24.

14. Anne Lamott, *Plan B: Further Thoughts on Faith* (New York: Riverhead Books, 2005), 55.

Excursus

1. Julie Stahl, "New York Officials Back Israel's Fight against Terror," *CNSNews.com,* 10 December 2001, http://www.cnsnews.com/ForeignBureaus/Archive/200112/FOR20011210d.html.

2. Michael Massing, "The Israel Lobby," *The Nation,* 10 June 2002, 1–2, http://www.thenation.com/doc/20020610/massing. See also Jeffery Blankfort, "The Israel Lobby and the Left: Uneasy Questions," *LeftCurve.org,* http://www.leftcurve.org/LC27WebPages/IsraelLobby.html; "Largest U.S. Delegation Ever Visits Ethiopian Absorption Center in Mevassseret Zion," *United Jewish Communities,* 13 August 2003, Shirl McArthur, "American Lawmakers Swarm to Israel During Recess," *Washington Report on Middle Eastern Affairs,* November 2003, 24–26, http:www.wrmea.com/archives/November_2003/0311024.html; Rep. Tammy Baldwin, "From the Middle West to the Middle East, a Wisconsinite's Reflections on Her Trip to Israel: Special to the Monthly Reporter," *Monthly Reporter: The Newspaper of the Madison Jewish Community Council* (October 2003): 1–2; Mohamed Khodar, "Sharon to Peres: 'We Control America,'" *Media Monitors Network,* 20 November 2001, http://www.mediamonitors.net/khodr49.html.

3. "Israel: Sharon Investigation Urged," *Human Rights Watch,* 23 June 2001, http://hrw.org/english/docs/2001/06/23/isrlpa97.htm.

4. Ibid.

5. Ahmed Bouzid, "Claim: US Newspapers Downplay Palestinian Deaths," *Editor and Publisher,* 23 September 2002, http://www.editorandpublisher.com/eandp/news/article_display.jsp?vnu_content_id=1705398. See also "A Tale of Two Killings: Observations of Media Bias in Reports of Palestinian and Israeli Deaths," Arab American Institute, www.aaiusa.org/PDF/taleof2killings.pdf.

6. Paul de Rooij, "The Scale of the Carnage: Palestinian Misery in Perspective," *Counterpunch.org,* 3 June 2004, 1–16, http://counterpunch.org/rooij06032004.html.

7. Lisa Nessen, "Nazlat Issa Demolition," *Pictures of Occupation: Articles and Journals,* 24 January 2003, http://home.earthlink.net/~plip1/artsWintSpring03.html#Nazlat%20Issa%20Demolition. See

also: "Israeli Troops Devastate West Bank Village Market," *The Palestinian Monitor,* 22 January 2003, http://www.palestinemonitor.org/Special%20Section/Demolition/israeli_troops_devastate_village.htm.

8. "Rachel Corrie Murdered by Israelis," *U.S. News and World News Digest: U.S. News Link* 2003, 1–14, http://www.usnewslink.com/rachelcorrie.htm. See also "American Peace Activist Killed by Army Bulldozer in Rafah," *Haaretz.com,* 2002, http://www.haaretzdaily.com/hasen/pages/ShArt.jhtml?itemNo=273498&contrassID=2&subContrassID=1&sbSubContrassID=0.

9. "Israel's Labor Party Swings Left," *CBSNews.com,* 19 November 2002, http:www.cbsnews.com/stories/2002/11/20/world/main530086.shtml.

10. Jerry Levin, "Israel's Apartheid Wall of Separation," *Mid-East Realities,* 6 January 2003, http://www.middleeast.org/premium/read.cgi?category=Magazine&standalone=0&num=807&month=1&year=2003&function=text.

11. "Dismantle the Wall, Says International Court of Justice," *Amnesty International,* 9 July 2004, http://web.amnesty.org/library/Index/ENGMDE150682004?open&of=ENG-2D2. See also Richard Roth, "U.S. Vetoes U.N. Resolution Denouncing Israeli Security Barrier," *CNN.com,* 15 October 2004, http://www.cnn.com/2003/WORLD/meast/10/14/un.mideast/.

12. "Closures and Checkpoints," *Palestinian Monitor,* 2002, http://www.palestinemonitor.org/Special%20Section/Closure/closures_and_checkpoints.htm. See also "The Targeting, Wounding and Killing of Medical Workers and the Denial of Medical Services to the Sick and Wounded Are Grave War Crimes under the Geneva Conventions," *Red Crescent Society,* 4 March 2002, 1–14, http://www.israel-state-terrorism.org/medicalrelief.html; Arnon Regular, "IDF Checks Report That Border Patrol Beat Youth to Death," *Haaretz.com,* 19 August 2004, http://www.haaretzdaily.com/hasen/pages/ShArt.jhtml?itemNo=246742&contrassID=2&subContrassID=1&sbSubContrassID=0&listSrc=Y.

13. Henry Siegman, "More Sharon: Partners on a Suicide Course," *International Herald Tribune,* 7 January 2003, http://www.iht.com/articles/2003/01/07/edhenry_ed3_.php.

14. "Richard Perle," *Right Web,* 22 November 2003, http://rightweb.irc-online.org/ind/perle/perle.php.

15. Rashid Khalidi, *Resurrecting Empire: Western Footprints and America's Perilous Journey in the Middle East* (Boston: Beacon Press, 2004) 53.

16. Ibid.

17. Ron Suskind, *The Price of Loyalty: George W. Bush, the White House, and the Education of Paul O'Neill* (New York: Simon and Schuster, 2004), 71–72.

18. Thomas Merton, ed., *Gandhi on Non-Violence in Peace and War* (New York: New Directions Books, 1965), 4–5, 11. See also Joan V. Bondurant, *Conquest of Violence: The Gandhian Philosophy of Conflict* (Berkeley: University of California Press, 1967), vi, 8, 24–26, 32.

19. Merton, *Gandhi on Non-Violence in Peace and War,* 4–5, 11.

20. Bharantan Kumarappa, *M. K. Gandhi, Non-Violent Resistance: Collected Works* (New York: Schocken Books, 1961), iii, 3, 6, 384. See also Bondurant, *Conquest of Violence,* vi, 8, 16, 18, 24–26, 32.

21. Merton, *Gandhi on Non-Violence in Peace and War,* 26.